Hunger for the Word

Lectionary Reflections on Food and Justice

Year B

Edited by
Larry Hollar

LITURGICAL PRESS
Collegeville, Minnesota

www.litpress.org

Cover design by Ann Blattner. Cover illustration contributed by the artist Anne Iott. Interior artwork by Helen Siegl.

1   2   3   4   5   6   7   8   9

Library of Congress Cataloging-in-Publication Data

Hunger for the Word: lectionary reflections on food and justice / edited by Larry
    Hollar.
        p. cm.
    Includes bibliographical references and index.
        ISBN 0-8146-2920-2 (Year A : pbk. : alk. paper) — ISBN 0-8146-3008-1
    (Year B : pbk. : alk. paper) — ISBN 0-8146-3009-X (Year C : pbk. : alk. paper)
    1. Bible—Meditations. 2. Food—Religious aspects—Christianity—Meditations.
    3. Hunger—Religious aspects—Christianity—Meditations. I. Hollar, Larry,
    1948–

BS680.F6H86 2004
261.8'326—dc22

                                                        2003021080

Dedicated to

the people living with hunger and poverty,

whose courage and resourcefulness

sustain and empower our advocacy

Contents

Acknowledgments

This book would not exist without the generous support of:

- Kathy Pomroy, Jim McDonald, Barbara Green, John Crossin, and numerous Bread for the World activists, who provided the initial encouragement to undertake the project and valuable insights that shaped both the content of the book and choices about writing, editing, and publication;

- Ken South and my Bread for the World Organizing Department and other colleagues, who suggested potential writers for the book, picked up the slack when the book responsibilities intruded on my organizing duties at Bread, and offered daily encouragement to see the task to completion;

- The writers of this book, who were amazingly prompt in providing manuscripts and responding to comments and were profoundly dedicated to making this a valuable resource for the faith-based, anti-hunger advocacy movement;

- Bread for the World members Anne Iott and Helen Siegl, whose artwork enlivens the cover and pages of this book;

- Bread for the World and Bread for the World Institute, which granted me a four-month sabbatical to edit the initial drafts of the text and additional time and resources to prepare the succeeding drafts and final versions;

- The Churches' Center for Theology and Public Policy at Wesley Theological Seminary in Washington, D.C., which graciously offered me a position as Visiting Scholar and abundant resources and warm support during my sabbatical;

- Colleagues of the faculty, staff, and student body at Wesley Seminary, who offered helpful comments on the book's progress and ideas that supported both my spiritual and analytical processes during my sabbatical;

- The editorial staff at the Liturgical Press, who embraced the idea of this book as a way to link justice and liturgy in intimate and compelling ways and who brought this book to life, especially my very able copy editor, John Schneider, and art editor, Ann Blattner;

- My wife Karen Cassedy, whose strong support and encouragement through the years made this work possible.

Introduction

▪

This book and the two other volumes that are part of the *Hunger for the Word* series are for people who love to explore and tussle with the Bible and are open to being changed by a Word that constantly testifies to God's deep love and special care for the world's hungry people. It is for those who seek justice and who value liturgy as the way we praise the God who embodies justice. Reading these pages may be risky business for you, but it's also a hope-filled and "Spirited" venture.

The blessing of food and the need to speak out for vulnerable people who lack food are not marginal afterthoughts or occasional footnotes in the Bible. These issues are integral to the identity of those who worship the God of Israel and who follow Jesus Christ. In raising up leaders in the midst of famine in Egypt, in offering manna to the vulnerable Hebrew people in the wilderness, in blessing the Sabbath gleanings of hungry disciples, in feeding multitudes on a remote hillside—God's provision of food helps define God's graciousness and underscores human dependence on God for what sustains life itself.

Many books written in the past decades have highlighted the wealth of biblical references to matters of hunger, poverty, and justice, and the need for people of faith to respond and speak out about them.[1] Others have explored the richness of the cycle of biblical Lectionary

1. These include Ronald J. Sider, ed., *Cry Justice!: The Bible on Hunger and Poverty* (Downers Grove, Ill.: InterVarsity Press, 1980), 2nd edition: *For They Shall Be Fed: Scripture Readings and Prayers for a Just World* (Dallas: Word, 1997); Arthur Simon, *Christian Faith and Public Policy: No Grounds for Divorce* (Grand Rapids, Mich.: William B. Eerdmans Publishing Company, 1987) 14–29; *Economic Justice for All: Pastoral Letter on Catholic Social Teaching and the U.S. Economy* (Washington, D.C.: National Conference of Catholic Bishops, 1986) 16–32; Craig L. Nessan, *Give Us This Day: A Lutheran Proposal for Ending World Hunger* (Minneapolis: Augsburg Fortress, 2003) 19–38.

readings, noting the themes of biblical justice that emerge throughout the church's liturgical year.[2]

For those who may be unfamiliar with the word "Lectionary," the term means an orderly sequence of selected biblical passages which, when read day by day or week by week for two or three years, are intended to give readers a relatively comprehensive sense of the main themes in both testaments of the Christian Scripture. Daily or weekly lectionaries usually include passages from four parts of the Bible: the Old Testament (also known as the Hebrew Scriptures), the Psalms, one of the four Gospels, and the other New Testament texts (Epistles, Acts, Revelation). In this volume, "Lectionary" means one of the weekly, three-year cycles of readings that many faith traditions—Roman Catholic, Episcopalian, Lutheran, and various Protestant traditions—use today as a tool for preaching, study, and devotions. Not every parish or congregation in these traditions regularly uses the Lectionary, and some faith groups seek more freedom and openness to the Spirit for sermons and Bible study than the Lectionary's recurring prescribed readings offer. But an increasing number of churches are finding the Lectionary helpful, just as more churches are mindful of the structure and order of the liturgical year as a resource for the church's life.

As the various lectionaries now in use developed, compilers adopted somewhat different approaches to exploring the Bible, so the sequence of readings is not always uniform from one lectionary to another. In more recent times, efforts have been made to bring the various lectionaries into a greater degree of harmony.[3] The *Hunger for the Word* series engages the readings in two widely used lectionaries—the Revised Common Lectionary (RCL), a version primarily used in Protes-

---

2. Dieter Hessel, ed., *Social Themes of the Christian Year: A Commentary on the Lectionary* (Philadelphia: Geneva Press, 1983); *Share Your Bread: World Hunger and Worship: A Lectionary-based Planning Guide* (Chicago: Evangelical Lutheran Church in America, 2000); Walter Burghardt, S.J., *Let Justice Roll Down Like Waters: Biblical Justice Homilies Throughout the Year* (New York/Mahwah, N.J.: Paulist Press, 1998). Burghardt and Fr. Raymond Kemp have done significant work to revitalize social justice preaching in the Church, especially in Catholic settings, through the Preaching the Just Word program sponsored by the Woodstock Theological Center, www.georgetown.edu/centers/woodstock/pjw.htm.

3. Useful books that describe the processes leading to the various lectionaries and the challenges faced in compiling them include Horace T. Allen, Jr., and Joseph P. Russell, *On Common Ground: The Story of the Revised Common Lectionary* (Norwich, Eng.: Canterbury Press, 1998), and Fritz West, *Scripture and Memory: The Ecumenical Hermeneutic of the Three-Year Lectionaries* (Collegeville, Minn.: The Liturgical Press, 1997).

tant churches, and the 1998 Roman Catholic Lectionary for Mass (LM). The decision to use both sources in this book (although with a primary focus on the Revised Common Lectionary) reflects the broadly ecumenical nature of the Bread for the World movement and the wide range of faith groups that are working together to end hunger.

A gratifying number of Lectionary-related resources are now available, including valuable commentaries on the assigned passages; suggested hymns, anthems, solos, and other musical and artistic ideas; and liturgical aids such as litanies and prayers. Magazines such as *Christian Century* and *Sojourners* and compiled volumes of commentary offer weekly reflections that challenge Christians to take seriously the call to discipleship by examining the sweep of the Lectionary cycle of readings from a justice perspective.[4]

The book you are holding is different from these other resources. Let me explain how and why. The story begins with a grassroots movement of people of faith.

Bread for the World (BFW) is a nationwide Christian advocacy movement that seeks justice for the world's hungry people by lobbying our nation's decision makers. Its life is grounded in its 55,000 members across the country, who are, for the most part, associated with worshiping Christian communities—in thousands of local churches, on hundreds of college and seminary campuses, and in countless justice groups. These people are not just "donors" to a cause; they are also activists, writing letters and making phone calls to their members of Congress and meeting with their elected leaders face to face to urge more effective and compassionate national policies related to hunger in the United States and overseas. They organize letter-writing events, called "Offerings of Letters," in their churches, on their campuses, and in various groups, inviting others to speak out to Congress and the President. They also come together in ecumenical local groups and telephone-tree networks to organize events and prepare concerted and rapid response to action in Washington.

BFW members study the issues and act on what they learn. For these dedicated activists, lobbying Congress and the Administration in

---

4. Excellent resources are *Living the Word: Reflections on the Revised Common Lectionary, Cycles A, B, and C* (Washington, D.C.: Sojourners, 1996), and Rev. Noelle Damico's provocative and creative devotions, prayers, and children's reflections in the Lectionary-based resources for Micah 6 congregations that emphasize justice, service, and spiritual growth, accessible at http://www.pcusa.org/pcusa/wmd/hunger/micah6/.

Washington is not just political work; it is part of what they feel called to do and be as Christians. Advocacy is an essential facet of their lives of faith, like breathing out and breathing in.[5]

As they pray and study the Bible, Bread for the World members look to Scripture for insights into the importance of food in God's economy and for challenge and encouragement in addressing the world's hunger. From Scripture they learn that God's people are constantly urged to respond in compassion with direct and immediate hunger relief —charity—and also with a commitment to justice that addresses the long-term, structural causes of hunger—advocacy. Both responses are needed if God's vision of bountiful food for all people is to be realized. Bread for the World's role is to foster advocacy, working to change national policies on hunger.

For more than three decades, Bread for the World has published biblical resources that explain the basic call to Christian advocacy and that support specific legislative campaigns. But BFW members and other people of faith concerned about hunger say they want even more biblical grounding for their advocacy work. Pastors and lay preachers want ideas on how to speak in sermons about hunger and justice, knowing that when God's people hear from the pulpit about God's pervasive concern for hungry and marginalized people, they will be more bold in speaking out for justice. Pastors and lay leaders also want suggestions about how to make hunger understandable to the church's children during worship and how to find appropriate and compelling music about these themes. In similar ways, those who use the Lectionary for Bible study ask for provocative reflections that enable dialogue about ways to respond to God's deep concern for those who lack daily bread.

From these hungers, homiletic and reflective, comes this book. It is not meant only for Bread for the World members; rather, it serves anyone who values regular engagement with thoughtful alternative and focused voices about hunger and justice.

Forty-six writers with creative skills and varied perspectives— pastors, scholars, and biblically grounded lay members of Bread for the World from across the United States—contributed to the three volumes in this series, published over a period of several years and covering each of the three cycles (A, B, C) of the Lectionary. These writers

5. David Beckmann and Arthur Simon, *Grace at the Table: Ending Hunger in God's World* (New York/Mahwah, N.J.: Paulist Press, 1999) 14.

are drawn from eighteen different faith traditions and from a wide range of ages, experiences, ministries, and passions. They and the artists whose work appears on these pages agreed to forego royalties and compensation to make these volumes possible—a real gift to the anti-hunger movement.

Each writer was assigned a period ranging from one to eight Sundays or feast days and was asked to reflect on the passages prescribed for those days in the Revised Common Lectionary and, where different, the Roman Catholic Lectionary for Mass. Their ideas both represent and respect the broad ecumenical nature of the Bread for the World movement and the wider community of those seeking justice in our world.

The writers were invited to focus on how the passages for that day offer insights into God's call to respond to those who are hungry and poor, and the general call for God's people to seek justice and engage in advocacy in solidarity with people who are marginalized and vulnerable. Since many other available Lectionary resources offer commentary on the meaning of the words in the original languages and on the cultural settings of the passages, authors were asked not to replicate that information. Instead, I told them:

> Your task is to creatively experience the passages from the standpoint of one concerned about hunger and justice in our world, and offer insights, stories, images, and provocative questions that preachers, study leaders, and others would find useful in wrestling with the passages. I encourage you to write in a way that is stimulative and evocative rather than scholarly and definitive. Your challenge is to constantly have on the lenses of one who, by your commitment to Bread for the World, can see clearly to ask the question, "How is God speaking to me in these passages in a way that shapes my concern and stimulates my speaking out with and for people who are hungry and poor in God's world?"

Clearly, readings for some weeks in the Lectionary offer fewer or less compelling examples of connections with the call to justice for poor and hungry people than those of other weeks. But writers were encouraged to offer what insights they could, consistent with the demand never to twist Scripture's word to fit their own agendas.

Writers also were invited (but not required) to provide two additional resources: suggestions for approaches for children's sermons or other liturgical times spent with children, and examples of appropriate hymns and other musical or artistic resources that could be used in worship or Bible study. (See "A Word About Children's Time Reflections and Musical Suggestions" below for more information on these resources.) When writers did not supply them, other contributors prepared those resources.

The following pages offer a life-giving and affirming sense of Scripture's grounding in the struggle for fairness, justice, and love for God's hungry people. As you read these pages, remember that none of us can live without our daily bread. Food is integral to our daily existence. As people of faith pray, in somewhat different ways, the Lord's Prayer/Our Father together each Sunday, we affirm our reliance on God for that sustenance. Thus God's Word given to us each week is always about bread. May that Word be opened in fresh and nourishing ways to you as you read this book.

Contributors to this book present their own personal reflections on the texts. Their ideas do not necessarily represent the views of Bread for the World or any faith group or organization with which these writers are affiliated.

To offer your own justice-oriented insights and reflections on these Scripture passages or to comment on the contents of this book, please write to Lectionary Feedback, Bread for the World, 50 F Street, NW, Suite 500, Washington, DC 20001, or by email at lectionary@bread.org.

LARRY HOLLAR

A Word about Children's Time Reflections
and Musical Suggestions

Each writer for this book was invited, though not required, to provide three parts of the weekly presentation: the reflection on the Lectionary passages, the children's time piece, and the musical suggestions. All writers prepared the reflection on the passages, and their names are indicated in the byline in the text. Some writers also prepared the other two parts, while others decided not to.

If there are no initials in brackets after the children's time piece or the musical suggestions, that means the writer of the Lectionary reflection also prepared those parts. The bracketed initials indicate that another writer is solely responsible for those parts of the weekly presentation. The bracketed initials you may find in the children's time pieces and in the musical suggestions are: [GF] Garnett Foster; [LH] Larry Hollar; [MH] Marie Hanselman; [MM] Marc Miller.

The musical suggestions for each week point to hymns and other sacred music that highlight themes in the passages and the Lectionary reflections for that day. These suggestions may be helpful in preparing liturgies on these themes. In listing sources for these musical ideas, the intent is to provide one source in a readily available musical resource—a hymnal or songbook from the faith traditions of Bread for the World members—rather than list all the places the hymn can be found. You may find the same hymn in a hymnal or songbook you use regularly. Often the musical ideas are songs which have a distinctly social justice orientation and which lean toward more contemporary settings and words. This reflects the fact that many current Lectionary resources provide lists of traditional hymns related to the week's passages. Our goal is to suggest additional quality musical settings that are both challenging in their poetry and singable for choirs and congregations.

Each musical suggestion lists the title of the hymn or song, one hymnal or songbook where it is found, and the page number in that source. The initials used to identify these sources are:

Musical Sources

AAH   *African-American Heritage Hymnal* (Chicago: GIA Publications, 2001)

BH   *The Baptist Hymnal* (Nashville: Convention Press, 1991)

BP   *Banquet of Praise* (Washington, D.C.: Bread for the World, 1990)

CCE	*Cokesbury Chorus Book, Expanded Edition* (Nashville: Abingdon Press, 1999)
CH	*Chalice Hymnal* (St. Louis: Chalice Press, 1995)
EH	*The Hymnal 1982* according to the use of the Episcopal Church (New York: The Church Hymnal Corporation, 1985)
FWS	*The Faith We Sing* (Nashville: Abingdon Press, 2000)
GC	*Gather Comprehensive* (Chicago: GIA Publications, 1994)
LBW	*Lutheran Book of Worship* (Minneapolis: Augsburg Publishing House and Philadelphia: Board of Publication, Lutheran Church in America, 1978)
MBW	*Moravian Book of Worship* (Bethlehem, Penn.: Interprovincial Board of Publications and Communications, 1995)
NB	*The New National Baptist Hymnal* (Nashville: The National Baptist Publishing Board, 1977)
NCH	*The New Century Hymnal* (Cleveland: The Pilgrim Press, 1995)
NHL	*New Hymns for the Lectionary: To Glorify the Maker's Name*, music by Carol Doran, words by Thomas H. Troeger (New York: Oxford University Press, 1986)
PH	*The Presbyterian Hymnal* (Louisville: Westminster/John Knox Press, 1990)
PSH	*Psalter Hymnal* (Grand Rapids, Mich.: CRC Publications, 1987, 1988)
RSH	*Renew! Songs and Hymns for Blended Worship* (Carol Stream, Ill.: Hope Publishing Company, 1995)
SF	Jane Parker Huber, *A Singing Faith* (Philadelphia: The Westminster Press, 1987)
SZ	*Songs of Zion* (Nashville: Abingdon Press, 1981)
UMH	*The United Methodist Hymnal* (Nashville: The United Methodist Publishing House, 1989)
WC	*The Worshiping Church: A Hymnal* (Carol Stream, Ill.: Hope Publishing Company, 1990)
WOV	*With One Voice—A Lutheran Resource for Worship* (Minneapolis: Augsburg Fortress, 1995)

Garnett Foster

⬛

First Sunday of Advent

⬛

RCL: Isaiah 64:1-9; Psalm 80:1-7, 17-19; 1 Corinthians 1:3-9;
  Mark 13:24-37

LM: Isaiah 63:16b-17, 19b; 64:2-7; Psalm 80:2-3, 15-16, 18-19;
  1 Corinthians 1:3-9; Mark 13:33-37

"O that you would tear open the heavens and come down" (Isa 64:1).
Isaiah's desperate cry for God's intervention in the life of the world
seems harsh amidst the promises of beauty and peace of the Advent/
Christmas season. It is not what congregations want to hear. Sweet babies and caring shepherds are more to their liking. Yet the Advent season begins in lament, in pain, in feelings of abandonment, in longing.

The lament comes from those recently returned to their devastated
land, seeking to rebuild and re-create their community's life. The re-
turnees take some responsibility for their plight, aware that their behavior resulted in God's anger and punishment. Yet they also blame
their sin on God: "For you have hidden your face from us, and have
delivered us into the hand of our iniquity" (v. 7).

The cry for God to tear open the heavens and come down continues
to echo twenty-five hundred years later from:

- Palestinian children who are suffering from malnutrition because
  there is not enough food.

- Hungry and homeless people on the streets of the United States.

1

- Orphans of the AIDS pandemic in Africa.

- Nicaraguans whose farms are devastated year after year by drought.

Their cry goes up: "It seems hopeless, God; there is no way out. You do something, God. We have tried our best, and nothing makes any difference."

"O that you would tear open the heavens and come down" is also the cry of those who seek to do justice. It is the cry of the faithful who see little if any change in spite of their faithful letter-writing to Congress, their coalition-building. Advocacy for poor and hungry people seems to bear no fruit, and years of work seem to have no effect.

Mark, in this difficult chapter of the Little Apocalypse, speaks to those who are despairing and who find it difficult to remain faithful to God when God seems absent. Mark's wisdom is "Beware, keep alert; for you do not know when the time will come" (13:33). There is promise here that the Lord will come, and trusting that promise enables us to remain faithful and watchful.

We must also act as doorkeeper, watching for God's reign and awaiting that time when justice reigns, when wars cease, when all can experience "home." It takes keen alertness to recognize God's reign in our midst, especially when our culture tries to negate such awareness. Opening the door is crucial.

"O that you would tear open the heavens and come down." This plaintive communal lament shakes the beginning of the Advent season. The cry is one of realism—God often does seem absent. As with all lament, we experience joy and confidence from expressing our pain and longing to God. Only those who trust God enough to be blatantly honest are open to hear the Good News at Christmas: "And the Word became flesh and lived among us . . . . full of grace and truth" (John 1:14).

Suggestion for a Ritual with the Congregation, Including the Children

The Advent wreath is a relatively new ritual for U.S. churches. There is no historically prescribed liturgy for lighting the candles. Many churches either use the characters of the Christmas story (Mary candle, shepherds' candle, angel candle, etc.) or associate them with certain feelings of the season (watchfulness, hope, joy). An alternative is to remember with each candle those in our society who are oppressed:

Mary reminds us of pregnant teenagers; the shepherds, of those considered unclean; the Magi, of immigrants in our midst; Mary, Joseph, and the baby, of refugees. Layers of meaning can be added to lighting the candle by creative choice of meaning for each candle, meaning growing out of the congregation's call to do justice.

Children's Time

Introduce children to lament. They know feelings of anger at God, of knowing God as unfair. It is important that they know they are not unique in these feelings and that God accepts them . . . and transforms them.

Musical Suggestions

[GF] "If the mall is playing Christmas carols, why can't we sing them at church?" We often hear this suggestion in our churches, but preparation for incarnation requires lament and watchfulness. Advent carols help create and express this longing that is crucial to Advent preparation.

[MH] Change My Heart, O God—RSH 143

May the Mind of Christ, My Savior—RSH 285

Standing on the Promises—UMH 374

Live Into Hope—PH 332

As Servants Working an Estate—NHL 40, p. 84

Garnett Foster

◾

Second Sunday of Advent

◾

RCL: Isaiah 40:1-11; Psalm 85:1-2, 8-13; 2 Peter 3:8-15a; Mark 1:1-8
LM: Isaiah 40:1-5, 9-11; Psalm 85:9-10, 11-12, 13-14; 2 Peter 3:8-14;
   Mark 1:1-8

"Prepare the way of the Lord"—
this is the challenge of both the readings from Isaiah and Mark.

The exiles, or at least some of them,
are remarkable models of faithfulness. Babylon is comfortable, an easy
place to live. After forty years a number of the exiles have been assimilated
into Babylonian society, enjoying its
comforts. The importance of their
faith has decreased. Others intentionally have not become assimilated
into their captors' culture, refusing to let Babylon become home, because they know in the core of their being that God's way is not Babylon's way. Aware that they are theological as well as geographical
exiles, they intentionally live their faith in a strange land, even when
doing so sometimes means they have to rework the Torah and their
former understandings of God.

Babylon, as we see in the book of Revelation and in popular culture,
has taken on the symbolic meaning of a place of power, of comfort, of

ease for those who are rich and powerful—and a place of oppression and injustice for poor and needy people. It is easy to see parallels between the United States and Babylon: both are unquestioned superpowers, prone to arrogance and self-satisfaction, quick to create enemies to protect their own power.

Those of us who seek to follow Jesus Christ can easily become assimilated to our culture. How easy to be caught up in the need for financial security, for power, and prestige. Advertising creates consumerism. But our challenge is to live "in" but not "of" the culture, seeking to live God's way, not the more comfortable way the culture offers. Isaiah hints at the lifestyle that is required of those who do not assimilate into the dominant culture:

- Hope: For those in Babylon the hope is that God will build a highway —not merely a path—across the Middle East to bring them home.

- Ability to sing praise: Even in the midst of displacement, the exiles engage in doxology, praise, and thanksgiving. "Lift up your voice with strength . . . lift it up, do not fear; say to the cities of Judah, 'Here is your God!'" (40:9).

- Understanding of God: God is one who acts, who cares, who is paternal and maternal, strong and tender: God "will feed his flock like a shepherd; he will gather the lambs in his arms, and carry them in his bosom, and gently lead the mother sheep" (40:11).

The exiles resist enculturation by how they choose to live, preparing themselves to resist the culture's wiles. Those who remain faithful to the tradition today still need these disciplines of resistance: grounding in Scripture; support and accountability to a community; participation in traditional spiritual disciplines, such as worship and prayer; and seeking ways to act for justice.

In the passage from Mark, John the Baptist calls for preparation— the preparation of repentance. John is a transitional figure. His lineage is priestly, but Mark links John to the prophet Elijah by spending more time describing John's looks and diet than his message. In drawing this parallel, Mark recalls the whole prophetic tradition which emphasizes the community and not merely individuals and which makes deep social and ethical demands.

For John, preparing for the one to come requires "repentance." This is not simply saying "I'm sorry," expecting to remove a breach in relationship; rather, repentance (*metanoia*) involves a complete turning around and going in God's direction. Frederick Buechner defines repentance this way: "True repentance spends less time looking at the past and saying, 'I'm sorry,' than to the future and saying 'Wow!'"[1] Repentance is a complete turnaround in how one lives and acts, not merely in what one believes. John's baptism called people to live differently —choosing to leave their old ways and live into Gospel values, into the justice the prophets advocated.

Children's Time

The two themes developed above can be used effectively with children:

To prepare: Amidst all the cultural preparation for Christmas, children can be led to explore how we prepare for Jesus' birth, how we open our lives to the one who is to come.

To repent: Children quickly learn to say "I'm sorry" as a way of pacifying adults and friends. They know it often has no meaning, and there is no intent to change. Discuss repentance as changing the way one behaves.

Musical Suggestions

[GF] "Prepare ye the way of the Lord" from *Godspell* calls for a parade as part of preparing for the one who is to come.

The ministry of John the Baptist is explored in the following hymns:

On Jordan's Bank the Baptist's Cry—PH 10

Wild and Lone the Prophet's Voice— PH 409

The Isaiah text provides the words for various settings of "Comfort, Comfort You My People."

[MH] But Who May Abide the Day of His Coming?—He Shall Feed His Flock Like a Shepherd—Every Valley Shall Be Exalted—O Thou That Tellest Good Tidings to Zion (all from Handel's *Messiah*)

Every Valley (choir anthem by John Ness Beck—Beckenhorst Press)

Change My Heart, O God—RSH 143

1. Frederick Buechner, *Wishful Thinking: A Theological ABC* (New York: Harper & Row, 1973) 79.

Savior, Like a Shepherd Lead Us—PH 387

Prepare the Way (Taizé Community)—RSH 92

Wild the Man and Wild the Place—NHL 36, p. 76

Garnett Foster

Third Sunday of Advent

RCL: Isaiah 61:1-4, 8-11; Psalm 126 or Luke 1:47-55; 1 Thessalonians
5:16-24; John 1:6-8, 19-28

LM: Isaiah 61:1-2a, 10-11; Luke 1:46-48, 49-50, 53-54;
1 Thessalonians 5:16-24; John 1:6-8, 19-28

(*Note:* This reflection assumes that you use Psalm 126 this Sunday
and Luke's *Magnificat* on the Fourth Sunday of Advent. See next week's
reflection for the passage from Luke.)

Joy is the cry of the Third Sunday of Advent. This day is *Gaudete* or
Laetare Sunday, consistent with the "O" antiphons traditionally used
during Advent. The antiphon for this Sunday begins "Rejoice . . ." Useful versions of this ancient liturgy are found in several modern sources.[1]

Scholars are not certain who wrote Isaiah 61, though it seems to be
one who has returned to Jerusalem and is part of the nation's rebuilding. The powerful words are perhaps the Spirit of God calling this person, in a way reminiscent of the call of the eighth-century prophet in
Isaiah 6. The substance of the call is to reappropriate the Jubilee tradition of Leviticus 25. This tradition is based on the sovereignty and holiness of God and challenges God's people to live socially and
economically in a way consistent with God's nature. The tradition's

1. See, for example, *Book of Common Worship* for the Presbyterian Church (U.S.A.)
(Louisville: Westminster/John Knox Press, 1993), and Hoyt L. Hickman, Don E. Saliers,
Laurence Hull Stookey, and James F. White, *The New Handbook of the Christian Year:
Based on the Revised Common Lectionary* (Nashville: Abingdon Press, 1992).

8

specific platforms are radical, calling for structural change in the society and not simply charity. That means protecting the environment by letting land lie fallow, canceling debt, freeing slaves, redistributing capital, and sharing economic power in ways that avoid a permanent underclass.

Isaiah's words are familiar because Luke 4 records Jesus' use of them for his inaugural sermon in his hometown synagogue. Jesus reads the Isaiah text and proclaims: "Today this scripture has been fulfilled in your hearing" (4:21). Whether he chooses the text because the passage reflects his understanding of his mission or because it is assigned him in the synagogue lectionary, the congregation reacts negatively. Turning from being glad to have a child of the church home, the crowd becomes a lynch mob wanting to throw the hometown kid off the cliff. Even though they aren't rich, they have too much invested in the system to want such a radical agenda imposed on them.

The Jubilee tradition that Isaiah and Jesus reappropriate is a clear call to mission for the Church today. It contains the vision for being and doing: for political liberation, economic reversal, and social revolution—a way of life that lets no one live without life's necessities. Just as Jesus incarnates the Jubilee tradition, the same words challenge today's Church, as Christ's Body, to reappropriate this radical understanding of life in community. And as with Jesus, such structural change can create lynch mobs of those who, even if not wealthy, have investment in the status quo.

If Isaiah's call to mission isn't hard enough, God speaks later in the lesson: "For I the Lord love justice, I hate robbery and wrongdoing" (61:8). Covenant relationship evokes works of justice, emulating God's central concern for the underdog and for justice. As Sharon Ringe writes: "The Jubilee traditions point to what happens whenever humankind encounters the factor of God's sovereignty."[2]

These Jubilee traditions motivated the Jubilee 2000 campaign, during which churches, synagogues, and other bodies around the world joined together to encourage lender nations to cancel or reduce the debt of the world's poorest countries. Such cancellation frees up monies poor nations would otherwise owe to richer creditors, allowing those funds to go toward food, medical care, and education for needy

---

2. Sharon Ringe, *Jesus, Liberation, and the Biblical Jubilee: Images for Ethics and Christology* (Philadelphia: Fortress Press, 1985) 36.

people. The Jubilee traditions motivated students at Louisville Presbyterian Seminary to develop a multifaceted response to hunger: enabling advocacy letter writing as the offering in worship, sponsoring a hunger auction to raise money for local programs that address hunger among children, and convincing the dining hall to serve only fair-trade coffee.

In contrast to Mark's understanding that we encountered in last week's lessons, the writer of the Gospel of John presents John the Baptist, not as the one calling for repentance, but as a witness. The one who comes baptizing denies being Elijah or the Christ or a prophet; rather, he comes to prepare and give testimony—to witness.

For many Christians committed to living faithfully, giving verbal testimony or witness is difficult and often feels presumptuous. Yet John becomes the voice of promise, in a sense the voice of Scripture. He calls people to see and understand differently and to acknowledge the Word's importance.

But John also knows how important it is to live that witness, embodying one's words. When John from prison asks Jesus if he is "the one who is to come," Jesus suggests that John look at what he does: the blind receive sight, the lame walk, the deaf hear, the poor have Good News preached (Matt 11:2-6—again echoes of Isaiah 61). Deeds as well as words are testimony and witness.

Individuals and communities today seek to reappropriate the Jubilee tradition and give testimony in word and deed through:

- communities that embody a life together that is nonhierarchical and inclusive of all God's children, where the words of the faith come alive through experience;

- partnerships in which poor and wealthy people acknowledge their need for one another and share one another's gifts, insights, and material goods;

- life lived for "the least of our brothers and sisters," where none go without food or housing;

- acknowledgment of the Christ encountered in those who are poor and hurting.

In such transformational living there is "a garland instead of ashes, the oil of gladness instead of mourning" (Isa 61:3). The cry of the Third Sunday of Advent arises: Rejoice!

Children's Time

Rejoicing and witnessing are both appropriate themes for children. Since our children live in a society in which many seek joy through consumerism, find ways to explain how and why joy is the central feeling of Christmas. Try exploring this while creating a litany in which the children respond "Rejoice" to each declaration.

Many children are self-reflective enough to look at their own lives as a witness, as testimony. Talk about ways you and they can do this daily.

Musical Suggestions

[GF] The "O" antiphons of traditional Advent liturgy tie today's congregations to others through the ages who have awaited the coming of the Christ in Advent. Hymns with a "rejoice" theme are most appropriate on this day. Examples are:

Rejoice! Rejoice, Believers—PH 15

Rejoice, Ye Pure in Heart!—PH 145, 146

[MH] O Thou That Tellest Good Tidings to Zion (from Handel's *Messiah*)

Live Into Hope—PH 332

Great Is the Lord—RSH 22

Awake, O Israel—RSH 259

Now Thank We All Our God—PH 555

Garnett Foster

Fourth Sunday of Advent

RCL: 2 Samuel 7:1-11, 16; Luke 1:47-55 or Psalm 89:1-4, 19-26;
    Romans 16:25-27; Luke 1:26-38

LM: 2 Samuel 7:1-5, 8b-12, 14a, 16; Psalm 89:2-3, 4-5, 27, 29;
    Romans 16:25-27; Luke 1:26-38

"Your house and your kingdom shall be made sure forever before me; your throne shall be established forever" (2 Sam 7:16). The Lectionary compilers chose the text from 2 Samuel because of its messianic promise, a promise important to both Judaism and Christianity. Although the writer of 2 Samuel would not have had Jesus in mind as the particular embodiment of this promise, the early Christian Church, in its challenge to understand Jesus, interpreted this prophecy as referring to Jesus.

Although usually seen in its messianic context, the story has a very human dimension. David seems to have healthy pangs of guilt that he is living in a mansion and God is still living in a tent. But could there be some self-serving impulse in David's desire to build God a house? Most rulers of David's time had a royal deity housed nearby. Perhaps in providing the Lord a magnificent house, David could extend his power and have God at his beck and call. Nathan's change of mind about building a house for God resolves into a critique of royal power and affirms God's freedom from human control.

Those engaged in ministries of social justice often wrestle with this tension. The desire for justice is a healthy response to a biblical understanding of God's desire for justice, but there can be self-serving elements there too. The choice of theological claims can seek to limit God's freedom to do new things, things that aren't a part of our agenda. What starts out as faithfulness can turn God's freedom into ideology. Government officials take office with intentions of working for justice but are soon co-opted by the demands of their constituency. Congregations find giving charity much easier than advocating for systemic change. Benevolence budgets often prevent discovering the newness of God, who is free and cannot be controlled.

The *Magnificat* in Luke provides a helpful tension to 2 Samuel's promise of a permanent Davidic line, reminding that God's promise to David cannot be reduced to royal ideology. Drawn from Old Testament canticles, including those of Hannah (1 Sam 2), a number of psalms and Isaiah, as well as the songs of Moses and Miriam in Exodus 15, the *Magnificat* is a radical song of God's turning things upside down. Often when musicians have put it to music, the music has been more a lullaby than a powerful, emotional proclamation of what God has done and is doing.

The one coming will bring about a great reversal and set the social order right. Verses 47-49 are Mary's personal thanks for God's raising her, a peasant woman from an insignificant village, to a place of honor. Verses 50-55 point to the great reversals God will bring about for Israel. As Central American theologian Elsa Tamez writes, Mary does not speak "of individuals undergoing moral change but of the restructuring of the order in which there are rich and poor, mighty and lowly."[1]

In reading the song, comfortable middle- and upper middle-class Americans quickly have to question where they fit in the picture. This baby might not bring good news for them, at least not the Good News they think they are seeking. Yet Jesus' followers are called to join this mission of justice, aimed at reversing the political order. This is good news for those who are poor, for undocumented workers, for the mentally ill on the streets of our cities, for those who have lost everything

1. Elsa Tamez, *Bible of the Oppressed* (Maryknoll, N.Y.: Orbis Books, 1982) 68.

in the dishonesty of the stock market; but for those who are comfortable, the canticle creates dis-ease.

Mary, in Luke's annunciation story, provides an intriguing model for the difficult discipleship of the *Magnificat*. We see reversal embodied in God's choice of a peasant woman from a town that has no biblical history. Gabriel's language is from 2 Samuel 7 and royal psalms such as Psalm 89, indicating that the child will be one with political power. No wonder Mary's response is fear, evoked not only by Gabriel's presence but also by the visitor's strange proclamation.

Mary is challenged to come to terms with God's intrusion into her life, with the strange and surprising ways of God, and responds, "I am the handmaid of the Lord." In contrast to Offred in Margaret Atwood's *The Handmaid's Tale*,[2] in which the handmaid is stripped of power and dignity, Mary chooses to co-create with God. Mary's receptivity to new understandings and her willingness to say yes without fully understanding the implications of God's initiative is the challenge of all who seek to be faithful to God's mission in the world. That ancient annunciation still echoes, asking for risk when all the data are not available, calling us to join with God in the work of filling the hungry with good food.

Children's Time

The annunciation story is a good one for children. Like most biblical stories, it has no easy moral but introduces the God who surprises and promises presence. Tell the story without comment and let it do its work.

Musical Suggestions

[GF] The service music in most hymnals includes various tunes to which the *Magnificat* can be sung. Miriam Therese Winter's rendition (NCH 119) is especially powerful because of her paraphrase. The Angel Gabriel from Heaven Came—PH 16 and To a Maid Engaged to Joseph—PH 19 are profound (though often unfamiliar) hymns based on the annunciation story.

[MH] Psalm 89: I Will Sing of the Mercies—RSH 111

Give Thanks with a Grateful Heart—RSH 266

2. Margaret Atwood, *The Handmaid's Tale* (Boston: Houghton Mifflin, 1986).

For Ages Women Hoped and Prayed—WC 143

Tell Out, My Soul—WC 350

Startled by a Holy Humming—NHL 19, p. 40

Glen Stassen

◼

Christmas Eve

◼

RCL: Isaiah 9:2-7; Psalm 96; Titus 2:11-14; Luke 2:1-14 (15-20)
LM: Isaiah 9:1-6; Psalm 96:1-2, 2-3, 11-12, 13; Titus 2:11-14;
    Luke 2:1-14

(Author's note: With tonight's passages and those that follow through Epiphany, let us reflect more fully on the shape of the kingdom of God. To me this seems essential work as context for our activism seeking justice for hungry people.)

The people have seen a great light (Isa 9:2); it is *the great light of God's presence*. Living in the great darkness of despair and oppression under the Assyrian Empire, the people believe that God is absent. Walter Brueggemann describes what they then experience: "And now light! 'Light' is regularly linked to the coming of Yahweh's 'glory,' that is, to the visible evidence of Yahweh's splendor, majesty, and sovereignty. This is the coming of Yahweh vigorously into the life of Judah where there had been only absence."[1] See Isaiah 60:19 (and cf. Rev 21:24 and 22:5):

> The sun shall no longer be your light by day,
>   nor for brightness shall the moon give light to you by night;

1. Walter Brueggemann, *Isaiah 1–39* (Louisville: Westminster/John Knox Press, 1998) 82.

but the Lord will be your everlasting light,
   and your God will be your glory.

The focus of Isaiah 9:2-7 is on God's presence in five ways: as *deliverance/salvation, light, joy, peace, and justice/righteousness.* We have these signs of God's deliverance because of the birth of the Prince of Peace. This child brings God's deliverance from our darkness, our mourning, our war and injustice.

Isaiah 9:1-7 is one of the seventeen "kingdom of God" passages in Isaiah that proclaim the time when "the zeal of the Lord of hosts" (Isa 9:7) will bring God's reign as God's deliverance or salvation (Isa 9:1-7; 11; 24:14–25:12; 26; 29:17-24; 31–32; 33; 35; 40 [or 40:1-11]; 42–44:8; 49; 51:1–52:12; 52:13–53:12; 54; 56; 60; 61–62). Jesus refers to these passages when he declares that the kingdom of God is at hand. Throughout these passages announcing the coming reign of God, five themes resound: *salvation/deliverance, justice/righteousness, light/spirit, joy, and peace.* These are the marks, the characteristics, the designators of the kingdom of God in Isaiah. Two more themes are almost as prominent: *healing,* especially healing of blindness; and *return from exile,* which means return from spiritual as well as physical exile from God. This is the most likely background for Jesus' proclamation of the kingdom at hand.

What "the kingdom of God" means has been a mystery to many people, but these are the five, and perhaps seven, scriptural marks of the kingdom.[2]

The same five primary characteristics sing with joy throughout Luke 1:5–2:20. Luke is announcing that in the birth of Jesus, the reign of God, or the kingdom of God, is at hand. It is *the joy of God's presence to deliver* that marks the kingdom of God both in Isaiah and in the Gospels. Luke 1:5–2:20 repeatedly celebrates the *joy* of God's miraculous *presence* and power acting to bring about Jesus' birth and deliverance of all persons whom God favors (Luke 1:11-14, 19, 25, 28, 30-33, 35, 37, 41-45, 46-48, 64, 66, 68; 2:7, 10, 18-19, 28-32, 38). The words "joy" and "rejoice" occur nine times in the Greek (sometimes translated as "found favor," "blessed," "gladness," or "exulted"). "Holy Spirit" occurs six times, and a revelation of the "presence" of God in which the angel tells them not to fear as a revelation or a vision is received six times. *Peace, justice and righteousness, deliverance/salvation, and kingdom*

---

2. See Glen H. Stassen and David P. Gushee, *Kingdom Ethics: Following Jesus in Contemporary Context* (Downers Grove, Ill.: InterVarsity Press, 2003) chs. 1, 6, 17, 22.

are declared in the climaxes (Luke 1:6, 47, 51-53, 68-69, 71, 73, 75, 77, 79; 2:11, 14). These are wonderful celebrations of God's delivering grace, announcements of the coming of the kingdom with all five characteristics of the kingdom, exactly as we expected from the kingdom-deliverance passages in the prophet Isaiah!

When Michelle Tooley was ordained by Jefferson Street Baptist Church in Louisville, an astounding assortment of poor people, seminary students, Latinos and Latinas, African Americans, people working against world hunger, and I cannot remember how many other representatives of different kinds of groups testified to the ways she had brought peace, justice, joy, deliverance, and the presence of God to them during her few years in Louisville. We each knew of her service in the group we were in, but we had not realized she had ministered to so many different people in relationships we had not known about. Spontaneously it came to me: A piece of the kingdom of God had passed through our midst, and we were all saying we had been wonderfully blessed by her presence. Now we were twice blessed—we could hear in those testimonies what she had done and could recognize at last what had been happening: some of the mustard seeds of the kingdom were right here in this one loving person.

Children's Time [LH]

Ask the children what it would be like to have a king come in the door tonight. We might think a king would come with trumpets and flags and a parade, but our king, Jesus, comes more quietly—but with great joy! Why are we joyful when Jesus comes? Invite the children to respond, and if they say it's because we get presents on Christmas, remind them why we give presents to one another. Talk about the deeper, more long-lasting joy of Jesus' love, and the love we give one another in gratitude for God's gift to us.

Musical Suggestions [LH]

Child of Mercy—GC 357

Lord, Today—GC 375

Sing a Different Song—NCH 150

I Am for You—GC 704

Glen Stassen

•

Christmas Day

•

RCL: *At Dawn:* Isaiah 62:6-12; Psalm 97; Titus 3:4-7; Luke 2:(1-7) 8-20
  During the Day: Isaiah 52:7-10; Psalm 98; Hebrews 1:1-4 (5-12);
  John 1:1-14
LM: *At Dawn:* Isaiah 62:11-12; Psalm 97:1, 6, 11-12; Titus 3:4-7;
  Luke 2:15-20
  During the Day: Isaiah 52:7-10; Psalm 98:1, 2-3, 3-4, 5-6;
  Hebrews 1:1-6; John 1:1-18 or 1:1-5, 9-14

Isaiah 52:7-10 and 62:6-12 are two more of the deliverance passages that announce the reign of God in Isaiah. Hence we see again
the five characteristics of the coming reign of God, the coming deliverance that God will bring: peace, salvation, joy, justice, and God's
presence. Isaiah 62:8-9 announces justice: the justice that powerful
enemies will no longer take food away from hungry people. So, too,
Isaiah 61, the great passage of Jubilee deliverance that Jesus often
quoted, three times announces righteousness (61:3, 10, 11). "Righteousness" here (or "saving justice" in the New Jerusalem Bible) is a
translation of *tsedaqah,* which appears so often in the Old Testament in
synonymous parallelism with *mishpat,* "justice." It means delivering
justice that restores community. It means the kind of justice whose
norm is the Lord, who hears the cries of oppressed people and sees
their need with compassion, delivering them from oppression and into
a community of covenant justice. Such delivering justice is one of the
five marks of the kingdom of God in Isaiah and in Jesus' confrontations

with the powers of his day, the high priests, elders, Sanhedrin, wealthy, Herodians, and their ideological supporters, the scribes and Pharisees. In contrast to them, Jesus practices the kind of justice that delivers outcasts from exclusion and into covenant community, that feeds hungry ones and delivers people from violence.

Luke 2:1-20 is not simply a beautiful story, and certainly not just a sentimental one. It is highly realistic. "Emperor Augustus" is the Caesar, the Roman imperialistic ruler over Israel against its will. The purpose of the census in which all must be registered is to tax everyone to support the Roman Empire's oppressive structures. Israel's people deeply resent this; this census, or the previous one, caused Jews to undertake a major rebellion against Rome. According to Josephus, the beginning of the Zealot movement is bound up with a Roman census. Mary's long trip to Bethlehem to be registered, while she is nine months pregnant, is her forced and very uncomfortable compliance with an unjust and oppressive decree. Because those laws are a sign of oppression, her journey is a testimony against imperial domination; yet because she obeys this unjust requirement, her trip also is testimony against the violence of Zealot guerrilla warfare.

What we have traditionally translated as "no room in the inn" is better "no room in the house." Luke 10:34 uses another word when it really means "inn." Still, there being no room is a sign of a lack of hospitality to poor people; had she and Joseph been wealthy, we can imagine room would have been found. The birth in the stall with the animals (and without anesthesia and antiseptics) is not a sentimental labor without real pain. Other signs point to their poverty. Their later offering of a pair of pigeons at Jesus' presentation in the Temple (Luke 2:24) is the offering designated for those who are poor. The shepherds who visit are humble folk, workers who served as night watchmen. It is a story about people of humility and poverty, oppressed by the Roman Empire, forced to make a hard trip just before giving birth. In the midst of this injustice, God's light shines, God begins to bring deliverance, salvation, joy, peace and justice/righteousness. It is a story of God's delivering justice coming to all those who are humble and poor.[1]

Christmas is not a sentimental story. It is the historical drama of God's coming and being present to those oppressed and depressed,

---

1. See François Bovon, *Das Evangelium Nach Lukas 1:1–9:50* (Zürich: Benziger und Neukirchener Verlag, 1989) 118.

those poor and marginalized, those who need justice and righteousness and peace and who need God's presence and God's deliverance. The joy is real; it is presence in the midst of humble reality.

If this is what Christmas means, should we celebrate it by an arduous practice of consumerism, seeking gifts for those who already have much? Consider doing what one family does: they draw names so that each person gets one gift, and with the money saved, they designate donations to groups that minister to poor people and work for peace. Make a simple manger scene, clip out some articles about the suffering of real people in our world and about groups that bring God's delivering justice, and put the donation envelopes by the manger scene. Then share stories about the light that some of these groups bring to people with real need, and close by reading Luke 2:1-20.

Children's Time [LH]

Use the time with the children to describe the alternative approach to Christmas giving mentioned in the last paragraph of the reflection above. See what their insights may be about how they would experience such a Christmas. What would it mean to make Christmas morning a time for sharing with people we do not know, who live far away, who may have very few possessions but, like us, are children of God? How would that enrich our sense of honoring the baby Jesus? What would we miss?

Musical Suggestions [LH]

God Reigns o'er All the Earth—NCH 21

Womb of Life—FWS 2046

In the Bleak Midwinter—UMH 221

Glen Stassen

⬛

First Sunday after Christmas

⬛

RCL: Isaiah 61:10–62:3; Psalm 148; Galatians 4:4-7; Luke 2:22-40
LM: *(Holy Family)* Sirach 3:2-6, 12-14; Psalm 128:1-2, 3, 4-5;
   Colossians 3:12-21 or 3:12-17; Luke 2:22-40 or 2:22, 39-40

Isaiah 61:10–62:3 is again one of the "reign of God" passages in Isaiah, giving the context for "the kingdom of God" or "the reign of God" at the heart of Jesus' Good News. Even in this brief excerpt from the larger passage, we see three of the characteristics of God's reign: joy or rejoicing, salvation or deliverance, and righteousness or justice ("saving justice" in the New Jerusalem Bible). The delivering justice that frees those who are poor and oppressed from poverty, exclusion, domination, and violence is an essential mark of God's kingdom.

Luke 2:22-40 is the story of Simeon and Anna blessing Jesus. Again we see the theme of justice: Simeon is a just man (*dikaios,* v. 25). And Jesus' parents give what is authorized for those who are poor—a pair of turtledoves or two young pigeons (v. 24)—symbolizing God's presence with and deliverance of poor people through Jesus. We see three other marks of the kingdom: God's presence as Holy Spirit three times; God's peace in verse 29; and the inclusion of the Gentiles in verses 31-32. The prophet Anna's blessing proclaims God's deliverance, salvation, or redemption. The fifth characteristic of the reign of God is joy, and surely the whole story is a story of joy at God's presence in Jesus, coming to deliver. Furthermore, the Greek word for "joy," *charis,* is in the concluding verse (v. 40), translated as "favor." So once again we have all five marks of the reign of God, including delivering justice. How can we possibly acknowledge the birth of Jesus, our Redeemer, without celebrating God's delivering justice for poor and outcast people, those who are dominated and victims of violence? How can we celebrate the coming of Jesus without some incarnational action to restore homeless people to community?

As Simeon and Anna were in their old age, my own parents died when they were "of a great age," each right around age 93. From our childhood and throughout life they gave their blessing to my sister and me whenever we participated in struggles for justice. One of life's wonderful surprises was when I joined with others from Durham, North Carolina, and rode the bus up to Washington for the March on Washington, when Martin Luther King, Jr., delivered his "I have a dream" speech. As I was walking among the hundreds of thousands there, lo and behold, I saw my own sister also marching. I had not known she was coming. Our parents brought us up right by their compassion for those discriminated against and by their blessing our small efforts for delivering justice. There was my sister! We walked a ways together, and, lo and behold, there was our dad! We had not known he was coming! Until the very end of his life, and even in the last half hour of his life, he was still speaking and exhibiting love and compassion, and blessing us for our efforts. There is no way I can put into words how very important those two memories are for me, what depth of joy they give, in a deep and permanent kind of way.

The ways in which parents bless their children and what they bless them for are so utterly important to the children and to their contribution to the lives of others whom they touch.

Bring them up to fear the Lord, which is the beginning of wisdom (Sir 1:14). Teach them, "Happy are all who fear the Lord, who walk in the ways of God" (Ps 128:1, NAB). Let this be the inheritance you give them: "God has sent the Spirit of his Son into our hearts, crying, 'Abba! Father!' So you are no longer a slave but a child, and if a child then also an heir, through God" (Gal 4:6-7). Let them inherit from you compassion, love, and the peace of Christ (Col 3:12-15).

Children's Time [LH]

Take time to think about the passages mentioned in the last paragraph of the reflection above, words of Scripture that suggest how we bring up our children so that God is deeply part of their lives. Consider how your parents and others helped shape you for your life of faith. Share a story—like Glen Stassen's of unexpectedly encountering his sister and father in a march for justice—that reassures young people that parents and congregation members share responsibility for reminding them that Jesus loves them and that God will be an enduring part of their lives.

Musical Suggestions [LH]

What Gift Can We Bring—UMC 87

How Good It Is—GC 727

Now Let Your Servant Go—GC 776

Glen Stassen

Second Sunday after Christmas

RCL: Jeremiah 31:7-14 or Sirach 24:1-12; Psalm 147:12-20;
    Ephesians 1:3-14; John 1:(1-9) 10-18
LM: Sirach 24:1-2, 8-12; Psalm 147:12-13, 14-15, 19-20;
    Ephesians 1:3-6, 15-18; John 1:1-18 or 1:1-5, 9-14

Just as Luke sets the ministry and deliverance of Jesus in the context of Isaiah's deliverance passages, so the Gospel of John sets Jesus in God's deliverance of the cosmos from formlessness and void into light and darkness and into life for all creatures. "The light shines in the darkness, and the darkness did not overcome it" (1:5) offers an image of God shining the light in the midst of the darkness of deep space in Genesis 1:2-5. Likewise, Jesus brings God's light into the midst of Israel's darkness as they struggle under captivity and without prophets; and he brings light in the midst of the darkness of our present world of need and greed.

"We have seen his glory, the glory as of a father's only son" (1:14). "Glory" here has the sense of light, in the brightness, radiance, or splendor of God's revelation. So it, too, connects with the emphasis on "light" as the revealed presence of God (1:5). The passage climaxes at verse 23 with John the Baptist quoting Isaiah 43 about God's delivering reign.

In Luke we saw the birth of Jesus as the light of God's deliverance. So here in John, with different vocabulary and different reference, we see Jesus bringing the light of God's presence. Jesus is God's true light that enlightens everyone (1:4-5, 9; 8:12; 12:46). The key is whether we receive the light, whether we believe that here God is revealed, whether we hear these sayings and do them, whether we walk in the light (12:35-36, 47-48; 1 John 1:6-7). So also in Jesus: it is not only that Jesus is the Son of God who was with God "before the world was made" but also that Jesus is the one who did the work God gave him to do, in his deeds and ministry and teaching (17:4-8).

Throughout the Gospel of John, the deeds that Jesus does, and the deeds that we are called to do, are deeds of deep love. We are to love one another (13:34-35) and to keep God's commandments (14:15-16; 15:9-10). There is joy associated with that (15:11), just as Luke fairly jumped with joy at God's deliverance. John's Gospel continues: "This is my commandment, that you love one another as I have loved you. No one has greater love than this, to lay down one's life for one's friends. You are my friends if you do what I command you" (15:12-14).

Jesus' love was incarnational love, the love of becoming flesh and dwelling among us. So Dietrich Bonhoeffer, born of a prominent family, became minister to youth in the slum of Wedding; went to Rome to experience the heart of Roman Catholic faith; went to the United States to experience a life different from his comfortable home; and immersed himself incarnationally in the life of the Abyssinian Baptist Church and Harlem. There he learned from African American Baptists to appreciate the way of Jesus more concretely, learned to follow the Sermon on the Mount more sacrificially, and learned what oppression and racism mean experientially. Therefore, when he returned to Germany, he saw more clearly than any other church leader what oppression and racism meant to Jews. And given a chance to escape Hitler's menacing rule and to teach in New York, he soon returned to Germany, because he knew he must follow the incarnationally loving Jesus and be with his people as they struggled against Hitler's hateful oppression of Jews.[1]

My students who act with love and compassion toward those who suffer hunger and poverty are inevitably persons whose lives were shaped by an experience of incarnational immersion in the experience of people in struggle. As the Son of God came incarnationally to identify with those suffering under oppression, and as Bonhoeffer went incarnation-

---

1. Josiah Ulysses Young, *No Difference in the Fare* (Grand Rapids: Eerdmans, 1998) ch. 3.

ally to identify with oppressed people, is it not the ministry of the Church to develop programs in which its members go incarnationally to identify with those who suffer from hunger, poverty, and racism? From that will follow the kind of love that abides in the light of the world—Jesus, the Son of God—and receives the Counselor, the Holy Spirit who turns us from hardheartedness and apathy to incarnational love.

Children's Time [LH]

Drawing from Glen Stassen's comments about "incarnation," think about inviting the children to touch and rub the skin on their arms. Talk a bit about how amazing skin is, how all the parts of our body fit within it, and how when people see us, they know who we are by the way we look—they can name us because they recognize our faces. But note that our skin and bodies are not all that we are. The love we share with others also says who we are. When Jesus had skin and walked among us, he showed us how to love one another. Invite the children to hold hands—to feel the skin of those next to them—as you pray.

Musical Suggestions [LH]

Blessed Jesus, at Thy Word—UMH 596

O Word of God Incarnate—LBW 231

Born in the Night, Mary's Child—NCH 152

By Gracious Powers (words by Dietrich Bonhoeffer)—NCH 413

Glen Stassen

Epiphany of the Lord

RCL: Isaiah 60:1-6; Psalm 72:1-7, 10-14; Ephesians 3:1-12;
Matthew 2:1-12

LM: Isaiah 60:1-6; Psalm 72:1-2, 7-8, 10-11, 12-13;
Ephesians 3:2-3a, 5-6; Matthew 2:1-12

Isaiah 60:1-6, and all of chapter 60, are part of God's proclamation of deliverance, of the reign of God, just like the "reign of God" passages in Isaiah on the previous Sundays. See the themes of God's presence as light (60:1-3, 19-20); joy (60:5, 15); deliverance from oppression (60:14); salvation and redemption (60:16, 18); peace and righteousness (60:17, 18, 21).

These five themes recur so consistently in the "reign of God" passages in Isaiah and in the announcement of Jesus' birth in Luke, and are so central in Jesus' ministry,[1] that we should not emphasize one without the others. We should not teach the wrongness of injustice and violence without pointing to the way of deliverance. We should not teach the way of deliverance without teaching the presence of God as Holy Spirit, Light, and Deliverer/Savior. We should not teach the presence of God as Deliverer without a significant amount of joy that God is here, delivering, and that we lucky devils get to participate in what God is doing—even if at this time we have only the mustard seeds and not the whole bush. Thank God for the mustard seeds that we do have! They enable us to participate in the traces of what God is doing, one step at a time, one day at a time.

1. See N. T. Wright, *Jesus and the Victory of God* (Minneapolis: Fortress Press, 1996).

Psalm 72 incisively shows us the synonymous parallelism of *mishpat* and *tsedaqah,* justice and righteousness. When *tsedaqah* is translated as "righteousness" or "integrity," we miss much of the point. In our individualistic and possessive culture, we think of righteousness as an individualistic possession of high moral standing, which is autonomous self-righteousness. But that, the Bible tells us, we cannot have (Rom 3:23). Rather, it means a community-restoring process, not merely an individual possession. Its norm is the Lord, who hears the cries and sees the need of those who are powerless and poor, widows, orphans, immigrants, and outcasts, and also delivers them from the injustice they regularly experience. This is delivering, community-restoring justice. Psalm 72:1-4 shows this parallelism three times. To participate in the actions of defending those who are poor among the people and giving deliverance to needy ones is to participate in God's delivering justice/ righteousness (vv. 12-14). Speaking out to our nation's leaders—the task of Bread for the World—is part of this call to defend, deliver, and save the lives of poor, needy, hungry people.

Another part of this delivering justice is bringing peace. "From oppression and violence he redeems their life; and precious is their blood in his sight" (Ps 72:14). In this psalm *shalom* is translated by some versions as "prosperity" in verses 3 and 7. It means "peace," redemption from violence, as well as the prosperity that comes when we have peace. Notice that God is the Rescuer, Deliverer, and Savior, and here God does this delivering through a just government. (More echoes of Bread for the World's work!) Surely there also is a sense of joy at God's presence in this psalm as well, so again all five marks of the reign of God are present.

There may be no surer way to understand how justice and peace can break out in this way than by experiencing need and deliverance yourself. In his book *Eternity as a Sunrise: The Life of Hugo H. Culpepper,* Alan Culpepper describes how his father and mother, after being liberated from a Japanese prison late in World War II, were sent to the island of Leyte to spend a month in convalescent hospitals. During that time, Hugo Culpepper relates,

> I was standing in line one day waiting to go into an army dining
> hall, realizing that my aluminum tray would be loaded down with
> more good American food than I would possibly be able to eat. I
> noticed to my left at the other end of the dining hall a line of

hungry Filipinos forming, waiting for us Americans to eat all we
wanted and then to go out and scrape into these garbage cans a
great deal of what we had been served. Our stomachs had
shrunken to the size of a clinched fist, and we could eat only a
very little, and were not able to eat more though we continued to
be hungry in every cell of our body—arms and legs—and not just
in the pit of our stomach. As I thought about this, it seemed to me
that the two worlds of our time had come to a meeting point
within my own self. My body was still identified, as was my spirit,
with the hungry, suffering people of the Orient. A few weeks before we would have been better fed to have had that garbage than
the food which we were eating in the prison, but my stomach had
already returned home to America and was being fed the finest
food available.[2]

Sensing, as Hugo Culpepper did, that many of us live on the edge of
both worlds is the prelude to action for justice and peace in God's name.

Children's Time [LH]

Several of today's passages speak of following light to a new, joyous
place. Describe a time in your life when you've been in a cave and seen
daylight and followed it out, or figured out which way was north by
looking at the starry sky, or followed a leader who had a flashlight illu-
minating a path in the dark. Talk about fear and hope, about light slic-
ing through the dark to lead us on, and about how important Jesus'
light is in guiding our lives. If you can find a small cross that glows in
the dark, give one to each child and have them remember that Jesus
loves them in darkness and light.

Musical Suggestions [LH]

Lord, How Can We Feed a Hungry World (Mustard Seed Faith)—
  BP 156

Carol of the Epiphany—FWS 2094

Who Would Think That What Was Needed—NCH 153

2. R. Alan Culpepper, *Eternity as a Sunrise: The Life of Hugo H. Culpepper* (Macon:
Mercer University Press, 2002) 97.

Arise, Your Light Is Come!—PH 411
We Hail You God's Anointed—NCH 104
Kyrie Guarany—GC 581

Rev. Clarence Williams, C.Pp.S.

Baptism of the Lord

RCL: Genesis 1:1-5; Psalm 29; Acts 19:1-7; Mark 1:4-11

LM: Isaiah 42:1-4, 6-7; Psalm 29:1-2, 3-4, 3, 9-10; Acts 10:34-38;
Mark 1:7-11; or Isaiah 55:1-11; Isaiah 12:2-3, 4bcd, 5-6;
1 John 5:1-9; Mark 1:7-11

John the Baptizer is the figure calling the people to repentance.
Through him the country experiences a great awakening, a great movement toward God. Jesus moves toward his Father's will when he approaches John for baptism. This baptism is not one of repentance; Jesus
is baptized to participate in a popular movement toward God. In Jesus'
baptism we see that he finds favor with God. Isaiah 42 affirms that the
chosen servant, on whom God's spirit rests, is to bring forth justice to
the nations.

The gospel lesson is important for us today. How do we find favor
with God? We have just celebrated the Christmas season and witnessed
with renewed fervor the birth of the child Jesus. With the wise men of
the Orient, we have adored this child Jesus. But this Sunday we see
Jesus full grown, and the evangelist Mark tells us that Jesus finds favor
with God. As mature Christians, how do we experience God's favor?

In their daily stop at the post office, people find a thin man in ragged
clothes sitting by the door, asking for spare change. He asks when they

enter and again when they leave. This man is a daily presence in front of the post office doors. When someone stops to offer some money, he courteously says, "God bless you." Some help him, others do not. Many have probably ignored him, and more have probably helped him. But no one wants this poor man to become comfortable living off their spare change. He is a constant reminder of the people in our society who have fallen through the cracks. Perhaps he is the victim of years of substance abuse or a mental patient who has been displaced with the closing of state institutions. Whatever his past, he is present to all who walk past him. Each time people arrive at the post office, they have to ask themselves, "What will I do about this poor and hungry man today?"

As people united in Christian discipleship, have we made our New Year's resolution regarding our goal of feeding the world? Aren't we supposed to see the onset of the new year as a challenge to our very survival in the face of widespread hunger? Each year news reports confront us with the startling fact that millions of people die from hunger and preventable diseases. Have we, like Jesus in the gospel, sought out those movements in our society that seek to make a more just world? Do our calendars, appointment books, and personal digital devices have dates committed to efforts to make the coming year a better one for others in our global village? When our resolutions for the coming year make us part of the movement building the kingdom of God, where the hungry are fed, the naked are clothed, and the homeless are sheltered, we too can hear our heavenly Father saying, "This is my beloved disciple in whom I am well pleased."

Children's Time [MM]

Explain what New Year's resolutions are. Tell those gathered that these resolutions are usually self-centered in nature—to lose weight, to exercise more, to get a better job, etc. Probe what the result might be if the children asked Jesus to help them make their resolutions. Perhaps they might resolve to be peacemakers or to show love for their enemies. They might resolve to fight hunger, racism, or mistreatment of weaker, more vulnerable children. Or they might resolve to walk closer with God this year, to "see thee more clearly, love thee more dearly, follow thee more nearly." Remind them that this year, as in every year, God's resolution is to love, protect, and bless them.

Musical Suggestions [LH]

Come, Holy Spirit, Heavenly Dove—PH 126

Spirit of God—FWS 2117

O Radiant Christ, Incarnate Word—NCH 168

Crashing Waters at Creation—NCH 326

Brothers and Sisters of Mine Are the Hungry—BP 148

Rev. Clarence Williams, C.Pp.S.

Second Sunday in Ordinary Time

RCL: 1 Samuel 3:1-10 (11-20); Psalm 139:1-6, 13-18;
   1 Corinthians 6:12-20; John 1:43-51

LM: 1 Samuel 3:3b-10, 19; Psalm 40:2, 4, 7-8, 8-9, 10;
   1 Corinthians 6:13c-15a, 17-20; John 1:35-42

"What are you looking for?" is Jesus' question in today's Roman Catholic gospel (John 1:38). All of us come "looking" for meaning and hope in life, for encouragement and understanding of the Christian way to cope with our earthly sojourn to an eternal destiny. In the scenes that unfold in our readings today, we learn that the "extras" are "extraordinary"! This can help us find what we are looking for in the Christian message.

In movies there are scenes in which the main characters are highlighted. Often when these scenes are outdoors, there are hundreds or even thousands of additional actors known as "extras." They are not the stars, but they definitely enhance the drama. In today's question, "What are you looking for?", we are the extras. Often in the Bible, extras act as the very hinges upon which the door in the drama of salvation swings open.

John the Baptizer is the Bible's preacher extraordinaire, for he is the very heart of good preaching. John does not preach to make himself look good or to make God look good to others. But John's preaching gives the people of his day, and especially his disciples, a good look at God. John is one of those extraordinary extras, the one who tells two

35

of his disciples, "Behold, the Lamb of God" (1:36). John plays himself down so that the star of salvation, Jesus, can take center stage.

In the first reading today we have the story of God's calling another great prophet. Samuel is like John the Baptizer in so many respects. He is the only child of a woman thought to be barren. Samuel's mother is so grateful to God that she gives her son to the service of the temple under the tutelage of the prophet Eli. Eli preaches his greatest sermon and teaches his great lesson in simply telling Samuel, "It is not I calling you, but the Lord." Eli is another extraordinary extra, one who sets the stage for the prophet Samuel.

In confronting the world's hunger, our roles as organizers, telephone contact persons, letter writers, pantry volunteers, and providers of direct services to poor people make us extraordinary extras in the drama of life. As we struggle to set up networks of caring involving our churches, communities, and governments, we look for ways for our world to see each person on the planet as our brother or sister. As Christians we seek those places in our lives—such as Bread for the World and the hunger movement in general—where we can get a closer look at God working in our world. When we see every person as our brother or sister, we can say with John the Baptizer, "Behold the Lamb of God" in the presence of hungry and poor people in our midst.

Children's Time [MM]

Begin telling about Samuel's call, and a few seconds into the message have someone call you on the cell phone hidden in your pocket! You can even play it up a bit—might it be God calling you, just as God called Samuel? But no, it's just an usher, your spouse, whoever, calling you to ask you to do something. But then revisit Samuel, explaining that God does call each child through prayer, through reading the Bible, and in their daily lives. Imagine what God might ask them to do when God calls. Invite them, when God calls, to answer, "Speak, Lord, for your servant is listening."

Musical Suggestions [LH]

Faith, While Trees Are Still in Blossom—UMH 508

Lord, When You Came/Pescador de Hombres—GC 696

The Summons—GC 700

Rev. Clarence Williams, C.Pp.S.

Third Sunday in Ordinary Time

RCL: Jonah 3:1-5, 10; Psalm 62:5-12; 1 Corinthians 7:29-31;
   Mark 1:14-20

LM: Jonah 3:1-5, 10; Psalm 25:4-5, 6-7, 8-9; 1 Corinthians 7:29-31;
   Mark 1:14-20

Freedom to make choices opens up the vistas of human possibilities. Mark speaks of those whom Jesus calls to follow him. These are men who have freedom to choose. They are able to abandon their work of fishing on the Sea of Galilee and follow Jesus. Mark is careful to make the distinction in the second group Jesus calls, noting that the sons of Zebedee work alongside "hired men" (1:20). Fishermen have freedom that hired men lack. The hired men and the servants in Mark's Gospel are not free to pursue opportunities in their society and in God's kingdom when they are bound to their jobs.

When we (and many of our parishioners) think of work, it is often in terms of personal fulfillment, but most of the world works primarily out of a need to survive. Those working to survive often are not in a place to follow the Gospel as their hearts desire. Their concern is about food for themselves and their children. Yet we find tremendous faith in many countries where hunger and poverty are neighbors, if not a border within families' homes.

An adage that challenges our faith is this: Christians read the Bible as if they have no money and spend their money as if they have no Bible. Our task today is to read the Bible and see ways in which we can make a difference. We can support causes that will ensure that all persons have a boat and nets so that they can make a living and seek the more meaningful realities of human existence beyond food, clothing, and shelter. Having resources to make a living can provide a means for a fuller life, a life beyond the chronic challenge of basic security of food and employment. We are challenged to ask ourselves, "How does my spending reflect my abandonment of the world for the kingdom of God?"

A group from St. Anthony Church and other inner-city Black churches on the east side of Detroit decided to raise funds to drill wells in villages of the East African country of Tanzania. Each well costs a thousand dollars to drill, but it changes the opportunities and lives of all the villagers. In many villages the girls spend their day walking to rivers and lakes to bring water back to the village, while the boys go off to school. When the village has a well, the girls also can go to school. To raise monies for the Tanzanian project, which is connected to the Missionaries of the Precious Blood of Canada, the group thought that a gala fashion show would bring out the crowd. So they planned the fashion show and invited people to come and make the world a beautiful place. This different approach brought a new audience to the event. The models and creators were so honored to be a part of the affair that they also gave donations.

Each of us is challenged to realize the blessings that we have and too often take for granted. There are so many ways to help with our own talents and gifts. Each one can hear the Lord speaking to his or her heart about our brothers' and sisters' needs. God's voice can come to us in prayer during a church service or on the runway of a fashion show. Let us hear in a new way Jesus' age-old challenge: "This is the time of fulfillment. The kingdom of God is at hand. Repent, and believe in the gospel" (Mark 1:15, NAB).

Children's Time [MM]

Hold up a sign with the word "Repent" on it. Ask the children if they can define it, and help them do so. Then hold up other signs that speak of what we need to repent of: hitting other people, saying mean things to others, not caring about hungry people, lying, forgetting God. Assure them that when we repent, saying "Please forgive me" or "I'm sorry," God does forgive us because of Jesus.

Another way to illustrate the need for repentance is to place a small shoebox on the floor with the word "Me" written on it. Then start placing bricks, with the items above ("hitting other people," etc.) written on them, on top of the shoebox. After about four bricks—depending on the weight of the bricks and the sturdiness of the box—the box will buckle. Explain that this is what sin does if we do not repent. Then pull out a new shoe box with "Me" on it to show the new self, forgiven and renewed through repentance and the forgiveness of God.

Musical Suggestions [LH]

Two Fishermen—FWS 2101

Would I Have Answered When You Called—FWS 2137

Christ Is the Truth, the Way—BP 179

We Are Called—GC 718

Rev. Clarence Williams, C.Pp.S.

Fourth Sunday in Ordinary Time

RCL: Deuteronomy 18:15-20; Psalm 111; 1 Corinthians 8:1-13;
   Mark 1:21-28

LM: Deuteronomy 18:15-20; Psalm 95:1-2, 6-7, 7-9;
   1 Corinthians 7:32-35; Mark 1:21-28

Today's reading from Deuteronomy foretells a prophet to whom the people can listen without fear of hearing God's voice, which they believe would lead to death. Jesus becomes the teacher with authority who speaks of God's will without threatening the people, offering life and hope rather than death and horror.

The writer of Deuteronomy says that God sends prophets to speak God's word to us, and if those prophets do not do their job correctly, the consequences for them and for us are severe.

What a challenge this is to those who see themselves doing prophetic ministry in the world today. We are compelled to keep teaching, preaching, and organizing lest we die. We experience a spiritual death when we fail to prophesy to our society. Because many churches lack a prophetic sense in our day, people in our world are dying a physical death. Our silence as a prophetic church is killing us silently, and physically killing our brothers and sisters throughout the world.

A secretary in my workplace decided to go to Uganda to share her faith with the poorest and weakest people there—children with HIV. When she returned from her two weeks in Africa, our director gave her time to share the story of her experience. She had photos of the babies and told stories about the absolute poverty. She told how children died in her arms. The entire staff was moved. She also told why she went. Her missionary effort arose from her faith, and the Lord gave her strength to witness in the midst of an experience for which she was in some ways unprepared. Because of her testimony and witness to us, the department took up a collection for the children's home she had visited. The monies will be a miracle, going toward purchasing an incubator to prevent babies from dying. Yes, her testimony will literally give the miracle of life.

In Scripture, Jesus' powerful miracles inspire faith and overwhelm people with spiritual excitement, so it's no wonder the crowds run and tell their neighbors. Witnesses to miracles testify to their families, friends, and strangers. The power of their testimony brings ever-growing crowds to see Jesus and hear his message. The challenge to the anti-hunger movement today is to demonstrate to so many who are doubtful and lacking in faith that we have the power in Christ to be a part of the miracles needed for God's justice to break forth. Daughters and sons of Jesus Christ, we are called to demonstrate the authority of faith in our social justice ministry. And we are called not only to point out the facts of domestic and global poverty but also to make a difference in the midst of it by our prophetic potential. The readings tell us that our silence can mean a spiritual death for ourselves and a physical death for others. Our silence today would leave the world in the hands of unclean spirits.

Children's Time [MM]

Tell the children about Jesus' power. He tells a demon to come out of a man—and it does! He orders Lazarus to rise from the dead—and Lazarus lives! He takes enough food for a few, prays over it, and suddenly there is enough to feed thousands! Jesus is powerful! And guess what—he gives his power to you and me. We have Jesus' power. (You might even encourage the children to flex their biceps.) We have God's power to change things that are wrong and make them right, and to help poor and hungry people to be fed. With Jesus' power, we change the world and make it look the way God wants it to look. Always remember this: you have Jesus' power! As the children leave, encourage them to look big and strong, and if your technology allows it, play the *Superman* or *Incredible Hulk* themes over the speakers.

Musical Suggestions [LH]

Lord, Speak to Me, That I May Speak—PH 426

Wounded World that Cries for Healing—FWS 2177

"Silence! Frenzied, Unclean Spirit"—NCH 176

Together We Serve—FWS 2175

Rev. Clarence Williams, C.Pp.S.

Fifth Sunday in Ordinary Time

RCL: Isaiah 40:21-31; Psalm 147:1-11, 20c; 1 Corinthians 9:16-23;
   Mark 1:29-39

LM: Job 7:1-4, 6-7; Psalm 147:1-2, 3-4, 5-6; 1 Corinthians 9:16-19,
   22-23; Mark 1:29-39

Job's lament over his days of drudgery and his nights of anguish
ring a chord in our postmodern society. Job finds no meaning in his
work; it offers no personal dignity, since he compares his labor to that
of a slave. Job is disconnected from any feelings of personal accom-
plishment, as he presents the worst picture of a person trying to make
a living. And yet today many of us in the developed nations and those
seeking development toil daily without joy. We sleep on mattresses and
the earth itself, but we cannot rest our restless spirits. Job's cry for
meaning that will give dignity to his days and peace to his nights is a
cry that echoes in our hearts and our times.

Paul's message to the Corinthians is the antithesis of Job. Paul finds
so much meaning in his work that he rejoices in the word "slave," because he wants to work all the time. To one person, slavery is a life sen-
tence of joyless drudgery, while for another, slavery is a mantle of honor,
a goal to seek. Living to spread the Good News is the core of Paul's
joy. He lives to give everything—his talent and treasure, all he possesses—
to proclaim and promote God's kingdom. He seeks nothing but the
kingdom and makes himself a slave to it.

What a powerful message we have today for our times. Slavery, which we often see as the most degrading position in any society, has two faces—one that degrades the person and the other that liberates. For us in today's world, our work can degrade us or ennoble us. What determines this is our attitude. If we see our life as meaningless, our work reflects this. When we see the meaningfulness of our life, everything we do shares in uplifting this meaning.

Many people give up their weekday nights to sort clothing for display at St. Vincent de Paul stores in hundreds of cities. They do this work to have the stores ready so that poor people can come in on Saturdays to see what they can purchase for their children and themselves. Whether it is warm clothes in the winter or clothes for play in the summer, regular retail prices are too high for low-income budgets. Often monies are prioritized to put food on the table, pay the rent, and find transportation to work. The men and women, boys and girls who sort the clothing are doing that sometimes boring work to make a difference. They come into the stores excited about their opportunity to serve, happy for the camaraderie of other Christians united in helping to improve the lives of people in need. These volunteers have found the joy of St. Paul in slaving away for the Gospel.

Mark's Gospel resonates with the theme of service. In Mark's Gospel, Jesus' actions remind us of the paradigm of the Suffering Servant. This long-suffering Servant could take the attitude of Job and complain about the constant demands people put on his time. Jesus cannot even get away to pray, because his new disciples ask him to once again amaze the crowds. But Jesus is ready to serve because, as he says, "For this purpose have I come" (1:38, NAB).

Children's Time [MM]

As you begin, bring out a table, place some chairs around it, and put on an apron—you're about to teach about Christian servanthood! Invite the children to sit at the table, but keep one chair empty. If you have the time and resources, give them menus and start pouring ice water for each one at the table (you could also already have the table stocked with napkins, condiments, etc.). Ask them what you're doing— they'll understand what's going on. Now ask them who's the boss here—you or the ones being served. Remind them of the chief premise of a restaurant: "The customer is always right!"

Now talk about Jesus the servant—"I am among you as one who serves." Help them understand the joy and fulfillment of serving (as with Paul). Now ask again, "Who is the most important, the server or the one who is served?" They will be confused, and that's okay. The point is that just as Jesus served us through giving his life, we are now to be servants for one another. Now refer back to the empty seat at the table, a silent reminder of the hungry ones who never get to be served, who have no seat at the table. If you wish, you may end with levity, as you switch places with the kids and let them be your servant. Start asking for all kinds of ludicrous items, throwing them into confusion—a fun way to end a serious lesson.

Musical Suggestions [LH]

The Fallow Heart Is God's Own Field—BP 193

Jesu, Jesu—CH 600

The Carpenter—GC 483

We Yearn, O Christ, for Wholeness—NCH 179

On Eagle's Wings—CH 77

Rev. Clarence Williams, C.Pp.S.

Sixth Sunday in Ordinary Time

RCL: 2 Kings 5:1-14; Psalm 30; 1 Corinthians 9:24-27; Mark 1:40-45
LM: Leviticus 13:1-2, 44-46; Psalm 32:1-2, 5, 11;
    1 Corinthians 10:31–11:1; Mark 1:40-45

Old Testament passages such as today's reading from Leviticus pre-scribe how "unclean" people are a threat to the community's health. One role of religious leaders is to declare who is a threat to the community's well-being and likewise who is no longer a threat. Today's passage reminds us of the role Moses plays in the Exodus event when serpents begin biting the sojourners in the desert (Num 21:6-9). God directs Moses to shape a bronze serpent and lift it up on a staff over the heads of the congregation. When Moses assembles the people, all who look upon the bronze serpent are healed. A religious leader's role in ensuring the community's health is a most important one.

Today many religious groups and leaders take positions on social is-sues that affect the health of the global village. Together they decry racism, casteism, ethnocentrism, and tribalism, because these are social illnesses that continue to destroy the mental, moral, and spiritual health of our communities throughout the world. These leaders challenge us Christians to lift our gaze from our everyday agendas and focus our vision on the "bronze serpents" of social evil. These serpents of social illness are literally eating up millions of people. Until we gaze upon these problems, we will not be healed.

Paul tells us in 1 Corinthians to be "imitators of Christ" in not giving offense to people because they are different from ourselves. In the early Church Paul is the forceful bridge-builder between ethnic groups. He addresses the issues of difference, including cultural, ethnic, and master/slave issues. Paul is one to lift up the serpent from its unseen presence behind cultural norms and let all inspect it in the light of Christ. Without Paul's fearless bridge-building, the Christian faith would have been landlocked in a culturally parochial viewpoint. Religious leaders continue to have the role of leading us from where we are in our current understanding of racial, ethnic, and cultural difference, building bridges to shared futures as sojourners in God's kingdom. Then we get to be bridge-walkers on that journey.

Bread for the World encourages its local grassroots advocacy groups to bridge the gaps that are present in our society, and especially to address and heal racial division. This can only happen when bridges are built. The Detroit Metro Council of Bread for the World gathered local BFW members one May to observe Racial Sobriety Month, a program of the Institute for Recovery from Racisms.[1] The BFW group sponsored for its membership an all-day workshop introducing the idea and practices of racial sobriety. The group's leadership embraced the idea that "we have to be the change that we want to see." The goal of racial sobriety is making good people better by seeing each person as one's brother or sister. Enhancing the anti-hunger movement's capacity to bring people from various racial backgrounds into the movement is only one benefit of building bridges. Just as important is the spirituality of seeing each person as a brother or sister. The vision of racial sobriety gives us the eyes of faith to see the kingdom of God unfolding as the unity of the human family, so damaged by racism, is restored to community.

Mark's Gospel depicts Jesus as the servant of a new healing proclamation. In the Old Testament the priest declares who is clean and who is unclean. Jesus picks up the role of religious protector of the community's health and becomes the source of restoration. Jesus looks upon the leper and takes pity on him, because the leper sees Jesus as his last resort. Jesus touches him and makes a difference. The power of this action is not lost on the leper, who tells others of his experiences and expands Jesus' community.

---

1. For more information about the Institute on the Internet, go to: www.ifrfr.org; or write The Institute at P.O. Box 13559, Detroit, MI 48213-0559; e-mail: ifrfr@aol.com.

Jesus' healing touch speaks volumes to the ills of our community today. At one time there was a popular adage about the meaning of health in our futuristic world. The adage was that in the future, "illness" would mean "I lack love," suggesting that sickness comes from a lack of love. In this gospel passage the notion that love heals the leper is correct. Similarly, social ills persist because love is lacking, and their healing is the task of those who love. Religious leaders must reclaim their roles as protectors of the community's health in body, mind, and spirit. The mantle of the healing Christ is on their shoulders. We are called to support them as the human family seeks and finds healing.

Children's Time [MM]

Talk about choices that we make every day: what to wear, what to eat, what to do with our time, etc. We also make crucial choices each day: to mock another child or to encourage him or her; to hang around with children who are cruel or with those who are kind; serving others or serving ourselves (underscoring last week's theme). In the Gospel of Mark today, Jesus makes a choice: he chooses to help, to heal. In the Garden of Gethsemane, Jesus chooses to stay and face the cross for our sake, rather than running away to save himself. Encourage the children to be aware of the choices they make, to choose as Jesus would choose, and to remember that Jesus chose to help, to love, and to save.

Musical Suggestions [LH]

Wash, O God, Our Sons and Daughters—UMH 605

When Jesus the Healer Passed Through Galilee—UMH 263

Through All the World, a Hungry Christ—NCH 587

Come to the Feast—GC 503

Rev. Clarence Williams, C.Pp.S.

Seventh Sunday in Ordinary Time

RCL: Isaiah 43:18-25; Psalm 41; 2 Corinthians 1:18-22; Mark 2:1-12
LM: Isaiah 43:18-19, 21-22, 24b-25; Psalm 41:2-3, 4-5, 13-14;
  2 Corinthians 1:18-22; Mark 2:1-12

"We have never seen anything like this!"

Isaiah speaks of God doing a new thing. Putting water in the desert and forgetting and forgiving his people's offenses are such new things. Just as parched ground can become a watered garden, a people can become a source of praise when grace abounds for them. In this passage the temporal earth is renewed as the celestial promise is extended again. The prophet's message of a new thing being done makes a cursed nation a blessing for the world.

This gives us courage to pray for a change of heart in our society. Perhaps we can see the day when God does a new thing with us, a day when our dry parched hearts might become loving hearts with God's help. Can we imagine our hearts so filled with the love of God that no one is lonely in our neighborhood, no one is homeless in our town, no one is excluded in our circle of friends, and no one goes to bed hungry in our country and world? Let us pray that God does that sort of a new thing in us. Then we too can say, "We have never seen anything like this!"

People in the crowd surrounding Jesus in the Gospel passage are with him for different reasons. Some are there to observe what he will do for others, while some want Jesus to do something for them. Others are there to examine him as a phenomenon. In the miracle that their eyes can see, he commands the man to get up and walk. Yet the question remains: Is the greatest miracle that a lame man walks or that his sins are forgiven? Jesus' challenge in Capernaum is still as great today. Do we believe in God's forgiveness that we cannot see, over the miracles of God that we can see? Which miracle is the most powerful?

The world in which we find ourselves needs both spiritual and bodily miracles. Those who do not have food need a miracle of the body, as do those who do not have shelter or a source of healthcare for healing. The Christian community can be the source of this miracle, but we first need to see the miracle of the forgiveness of our sins. If we could ever see that spiritual miracle of forgiveness, the world could also see the global village get up and walk. Until this time, we as a human family live in a blind and lame reality. When we accept the miracle of forgiveness, all will realize the miracle of a walking, dancing, and praising world. Then we too can join the chorus of Capernaum, "We have never seen anything like this!"

Not long ago Christians worked and prayed for a miracle in the Jubilee 2000 movement for debt cancellation to lift the burden on poor debtor nations. Through the efforts of Bread for the World and Christians and other groups around the world, debt relief was approved so that countries deep in debt could have a fresh start. In this case the miracle of debt "forgiveness" was a communal healing of the lameness plaguing their economic development. It was the Christ of the Christian Churches saying encouragingly, "Get up and walk."

Children's Time [MM]

Read the first verse of today's psalm: "Happy are those who consider the poor; the Lord delivers them in the day of trouble." Did the children know that? Did they know that God blesses those who bless others? A parable in Matthew (18:23-35) describes the antithesis. This is tricky ground—we don't want to instill the belief that God works on some kind of divine rewards system based on cause and effect. However, the same God who does give us our daily bread is glad when we share our bread with the hungry. So, yes, we are blessed when we "consider the poor." They are blessed as well, and God's heart is filled with joy.

Musical Suggestions [LH]

What Gift Can We Bring—UMH 87

What Does the Lord Require of You—FWS 2174

O Christ, the Healer—UMH 265

From the Crush of Wealth and Power—NCH 552

Rev. Clarence Williams, C.Pp.S.

Eighth Sunday in Ordinary Time

RCL: Hosea 2:14-20; Psalm 103:1-13, 22; 2 Corinthians 3:1-6;
    Mark 2:13-22

LM: Hosea 2:16b, 17b, 21-22; Psalm 103:1-2, 3-4, 8, 10, 12-13;
    2 Corinthians 3:1b-6; Mark 2:18-22

Jesus constantly recommends new wineskins. Just look at whom he associates with and how he directs his disciples' spiritual practices. Working for justice and against hunger can draw forth the same reactions that Jesus exhibits in today's gospel. As Bread for the World seeks to make our nation's elected government leaders more responsive, a lot of this movement's time is spent influencing the policies that can lessen or (sometimes) worsen hunger. Associating with politicians who make federal policy is suspect in the eyes of many Christians in every faith tradition. Writing letters to congressional leaders is a form of lobbying, and some see this as too "political" for the Church.

Today's passage from 2 Corinthians reminds us that we are "letters" of faith. "You are our letter, written on our hearts, known and read by all, shown to be a letter of Christ administered by us, written not in ink but by the Spirit of the living God, not on tablets of stone but on tablets that are hearts of flesh" (3:2-3, NAB). What a powerful symbol for our efforts to continue the apostolic tradition, finding our "voice" of concern through letter writing, in this case speaking out to the nation's leaders. Our pen and ink can give a witness that our hearts are full of Christian love.

52

Today more and more religious traditions are finding their voice in the political process of lobbying for those who are poor in our society and world. Religious bodies are calling for a change in the "wineskin" of what responsible Christian living and faithful discipleship are in the world today. The "social" gospel of feeding the poor and providing assistance for those in need is not a new patch on an old garment. The social gospel has always been part of discipleship, though too often it is overlooked. After all, the Lord has been one to vindicate and bring justice to oppressed people since the psalmist's time (103:6).

Children's Time [MM]

Ask the children of school age, "Who do you sit with at lunchtime at school?" Obviously, they sit with their friends. Ask them if they know who Jesus sat with at lunchtime. He ate with the ones who got into trouble, who weren't popular, the ones no one else would sit with. Why did Jesus do that? Would we sit next to those whom no one else would sit next to? What would happen if we did? Jesus associated with and came to save all God's people. Invite the children to do as Jesus did—sit with the ones no one else will. By doing so, it is like sitting next to Jesus himself (as in Matthew 25:31-46).

Musical Suggestions [LH]

Hear the Voice of God, So Tender—NCH 174

This Is a Day of New Beginnings—UMH 383

Holy Spirit, Come, Confirm Us—NCH 264

All Who Hunger—GC 820

Rev. Clarence Williams, C.Pp.S.

Transfiguration of the Lord

RCL: 2 Kings 2:1-12; Psalm 50:1-6; 2 Corinthians 4:3-6; Mark 9:2-9
LM: Daniel 7:9-10, 13-14; Psalm 97:1-2, 5-6; 2 Peter 1:16-19;
  Mark 9:2-10

The disciples' question after Jesus' transfiguration is at the root of our discipleship. What is the meaning of "rising from the dead" (Mark 9:10)? The Christian understanding that death is a passage to new life is the core of our reality. The number seven in the Bible speaks to completion. The notation at the beginning of our Gospel passage, namely, that the transfiguration occurs after six days (9:2), indicates the completion of a stage of discipleship that prepares Christ's followers for their apostleship. Their mission is to go forth with Christ's message, though they are sworn to secrecy until the resurrection. With this knowledge, they have questions about the "rising from the dead."

The question before us is: What do we do when we have seen the light? When does our discipleship become an apostleship to the world? When we see homeless and working poor people struggling in our own communities, when does our apostleship begin at home? The newspaper headlines and leading stories in the electronic media underscore the question: When does our apostleship begin?

The voice of God the Father breaking through the transfiguration is clear: "This is my beloved Son. Listen to him" (9:7, NAB). We must be ready to respond to the Word of God we hear today. We no longer have a secret to keep about our salvation; in fact, we have a proclamation to share. In the reading from Daniel we see the end-time vision in which "peoples of every language serve him" (Dan 7:14, NAB). Those who seek God's kingdom are the Lord's apostles who gratefully serve him on earth.

Bread for the World members in Detroit, Michigan, are among those active in Freedom House, a shelter for indigent immigrants seeking political asylum in nearby Canada or in the United States. Initially focused on Central American refugees, Freedom House now offers shelter, medical care, and other essential social services to people from all over the world, many of whom are fleeing political and ethnic turmoil in Africa, Eastern Europe, and the Middle East. Offering this sanctuary is never easy in the midst of the anti-immigrant feelings that exist in our society, but Freedom House has worked to overcome the border patrol's initial suspicions and to gain the confidence of the legal system that immigrants must negotiate. Located within sight of the Ambassador Bridge, which spans the Detroit River to Canada, this harbor in the midst of our social storm offers a vision of "every language" serving him. This house and the immigrants and local volunteers involved in it are a living gospel of what it means to rise from the dead. We rise from the deadness of our denials of the tragedy in the world in which we live. We rise from ambivalence about poor people and the deadly good intentions that are never translated into good actions. Right in view of the U.S.-Canadian border, this shelter is a sanctuary of the transfiguration as all who come here to help and be helped transform each other. Visiting the safe house is a spiritual pilgrimage in which disciples of Christ today can surely say, "It is good that we are here!"

Children's Time [MM]

Retell the story of the transfiguration, mentioning the "dwellings" (or "shelters," "tents," or "booths") that Peter proposes. Explain that Jesus and the disciples regularly slept in these kinds of crude accommodations while they traveled. Talk with the children about their homes. Many probably live in fine houses. Would they like to live in a tent all the time? (Some might well say yes, and you may have to remind them of the sober realities of life without a house.) Ask the children if they know or have seen anyone who doesn't sleep in a house, such as homeless people. Give thanks to God for the nice houses we do enjoy, and pray for God's blessing for those who do not have a house. Also, give thanks that Jesus, shining with the foreshadowing of resurrection, will one day prepare a house for everybody in heaven (John 14:2).

Musical Suggestions [LH]

Sanctuary—RSH 185

Swiftly Pass the Clouds of Glory—PH 73

We Have Come at Christ's Own Bidding—NCH 182

Michelle Tooley

Ash Wednesday

RCL: Joel 2:1-2, 12-17 or Isaiah 58:1-12; Psalm 51:1-17;
  2 Corinthians 5:20b–6:10; Matthew 6:1-6, 16-21

LM: Joel 2:12-18; Psalm 51:3-4, 5-6ab, 12-13, 14, 17;
  2 Corinthians 5:20–6:2; Matthew 6:1-6, 16-18

Ash Wednesday signals the beginning of Lent, a season of self-examination and preparation for Holy Week and Easter, often marked by fasting and reminders of the sacrificial element of the cross for all who follow Jesus. Three of today's readings focus on the practice and intent of fasting, reminding us that spiritual disciplines don't occur in isolation but are practiced in the context of a world with great need. Voluntary fasting reminds us that the human body needs food and that millions of people are chronically hungry throughout the world.

Joel's words call for repentance and prayer. The day of the Lord, God's judgment, is approaching, and God's people, who are suffering for their unfaithfulness, are urged to repent and return to a gracious and loving God. God calls for outward signs of the congregation's changed behavior: tears, fasting, and mourning. Fasting reflects God's holiness and demonstrates repentance and a deep desire for a new beginning with God. God's compassionate response in verse 18 offers hope.

The passage from Isaiah also depicts God's justice juxtaposed with a religious community that practices fasting superficially, in a way that does not honor God. Quaker sociologist and peacemaker Elise Boulding says that we have a world with injustice because we have lost the capacity to imagine a world with justice. When we imagine such a world, we can work toward that image of justice.

Isaiah's author directly criticizes those who fast, reminding them (in verse 3) that they are greedy and exploit their workers. Who are the oppressors and the exploited today? We think of CEOs and accountants of corporations like Enron and WorldCom, who made millions while thousands of employees and investors lost pensions and life savings. We think of coffee farmers in Colombia, Chiapas, and Guatemala, who make fifty cents per kilo of coffee while consumers pay $3.50 for a vanilla latte at Starbucks. This passage prompts our reflection as we ask who makes the profit and how much profit is just.

Isaiah offers an explicit corrective for unhealthy worship practices, calling for concrete, specific acts of justice as an act of worship. These include sharing bread with those who are hungry, stopping oppression of workers, housing homeless people, clothing those without clothes, practicing Sabbath as part of the Jubilee tradition, ministering to relatives, and reducing violence. In *La Biblia para Latinoamerica,* Isaiah 58:10 speaks of economic choices: "If you give the hungry person what you would desire for yourself and if you satisfy the oppressed person . . ." (author's translation).

The question for Christians today is whether we treat this as a desirable but unattainable example of moral perfection, or do we make it our daily practice? The Abejas, a pacifist Christian community of seven thousand who live in small villages nestled in the mountains of Chiapas, Mexico, believe that Isaiah's vision and other teachings about justice should be practiced daily. These Mayan Indians have no power as the world defines power; they are economically poor and lack formal education, and the Mexican government considers them lazy Indians and troublemakers. The Abejas know the daily reality of both military and economic violence, which are inexorably linked. Economic violence takes the form of poverty. Their fertile soil grows corn and coffee abundantly, but since Mexico's signing of the North American Free Trade Agreement (NAFTA) in 1994, U.S. agribusiness has undercut corn prices, so campesinos' corn is no longer a viable product on the market in nearby towns. Instead of selling their corn the way they used to before NAFTA, the Abejas now use the two annual crops of corn only for their own sustenance. Since NAFTA, poverty and hunger have worsened in Chiapas, a state rich in natural resources.

The Abejas live in an area where the military has displaced thousands of poor campesinos, so this community has taken in hundreds of refugees hiding in the mountains. They have few material resources, but as the lay leader of the church said, "If we have two hands of corn, we give them one. If we have two tortillas, we give them one. We work with them on the land. It is what the Gospel demands of us. They are our brothers and sisters." The Abejas could respond to the injustice in their midst with despair, cynicism, or retaliatory violence, but instead they respond to oppression with prayer, fasting, and organizing for nonviolent social change. They do what they do because they read the Bible and hear God's call to radical discipleship, to love their neighbors, and to be peacemakers in the context of injustice.

Matthew continues the conversation on fasting with Jesus' admonition to fast, give alms, and pray in secret. Jesus must be addressing a context like Isaiah's, where these religious disciplines are practiced for public approval rather than as signs of genuine repentance and changed behavior. We think today of newspaper accounts of charity balls and the attention given to the philanthropy of millionaires. Jesus ends with advice not to store up treasures on earth, since that indicates where your heart is. As we consider how we store treasures, often in the form of savings accounts and retirement funds, what and whom are we supporting? What kinds of corporations do our mutual funds support, and how do our banks invest our funds? Many people choose to invest in socially responsible funds or use community development banks, like the Community Development Bank in Louisville or South Shore Bank in Chicago.

In 2 Corinthians, Paul recounts some of the locations where faithful disciples will be, doing Christ's work. These remind me of Franz Jäggerstätter, who was killed rather than pledge allegiance to Hitler in World War II; Cesar Chavez, who spent time in prison and in protests for his work with migrant workers in California; and Dorothy Day, who began the Catholic Worker Movement during the Depression and practiced voluntary poverty.

Children's Time

Materials: Pictures from Sunday School

Ask the children's Sunday School teachers to do an art project with Isaiah 58. First talk about the setting of Isaiah 58, particularly verses

2-12. Tell the children that the religious people in Judah were talking about following God, but they weren't doing good to others. With crayons and markers, have the children do pictures of two scenes: how God doesn't want us to treat others (verses 3-4) and then how God wants us to treat others (verse 7).

Bring the pictures to church, and during the children's message talk about the lessons from chapter 58. Talk about how the people of Judah acted, coming to worship and making a big deal about following God while not paying workers enough for them to feed their families, and also fighting and quarreling. Read verses 6-7 and verse 10 and ask the children what kinds of things please God. Mention how good it is for children and adults to come to Sunday School and church, but that God also wants us to love people and help others every day, not just when we come to church.

Musical Suggestions

Amazing Grace! How Sweet the Sound—BP 105

He Came to Set Us Free—BP 153

Guide Me, O Thou Great Jehovah—BH 56

God, Our Author and Creator—BH 590

Michelle Tooley

First Sunday of Lent

RCL: Genesis 9:8-17; Psalm 25:1-10; 1 Peter 3:18-22; Mark 1:9-15
LM: Genesis 9:8-15; Psalm 25:4-5, 6-7, 8-9; 1 Peter 3:18-22;
    Mark 1:12-15

In the midst of a world with pain and suffering, we need God's de-livering love. After a passage that affirms suffering as a consequence of doing right, the reading from 1 Peter focuses on Jesus' suffering. The two Old Testament passages speak of God's deliverance—first with Noah's family, leading to God's promise, then with the psalmist's plea that acknowledges God's steadfast love and mercy. The gospel continues the theme of delivering love, with Jesus announcing the reign of God.

The passage from Genesis begins with God's initiating an uncondi-tional covenant with Noah, his descendants, and all living creatures, insisting that a flood will never again destroy the earth. Yet today natu-ral disasters, or "acts of God," whether floods, earthquakes, tsunamis, or hurricanes, still leave destruction in their wake. In 1998 Hurricane Mitch hit Central America, leaving thousands hungry and homeless and millions of dollars of infrastructure destroyed. News accounts reported that hundreds of people died, many by mudslides in Nicaragua and Honduras. But the real killer was not Hurricane Mitch—it was poverty. These deaths occurred, not because of hurricanes or mudslides, but because poverty forced people to build flimsy dwellings on unstable, fragile land. The United States has weathered much stronger hurri-canes with few fatalities. Hurricane Mitch hit nations already severely weakened by poverty. Governments like Nicaragua's, with the world's highest per capita foreign debt, struggle to repay their debt to governments and international financial institutions like the World Bank and the International Monetary Fund, when they should be investing those resources in the social needs of their country.

Psalm 25 alludes three times to God's steadfast love, which knows no bounds and is not conditioned on political party, religious tradition, economic class, race, nationality, or gender. In today's world, peasant farmers in Haiti question if they live in a nation that God has forgotten, and mothers in sub-Saharan Africa watch their children die of AIDS because they cannot afford medicine. In such a world, how are U.S. Christians practicing God's steadfast love? We can embody God's love for hungry people by giving funds through hunger organizations or by volunteering at a soup kitchen or food pantry. Another way to practice God's steadfast love is by using our public voices to advocate for hungry people in our nation and world. In several recent years, Bread for the World members and churches wrote letters to Congress on behalf of our sisters and brothers in Africa, urging Congress to add billions of dollars to our foreign aid budget for poverty-focused development in sub-Saharan Africa. The increase in aid would be this nation's share to help Africa cut hunger in half.

Christians in many countries throughout the world draw hope from 1 Peter 3. The ten verses preceding our reading today give counsel and hope to those who are suffering; then verses 18-22 continue the message with a reflection on Christ's suffering. Hector Mondragón, a Mennonite economist in Colombia, heard God's call to work against poverty after visiting a Bogotá slum when he was thirteen years old. In spite of prison, torture, and death threats, he continues to denounce economic injustice and to call for a negotiated political end to a forty-year war that exacerbates Colombia's poverty. Christians can stand in solidarity with people like Hector, who are suffering because of their courageous actions to end injustice. Through prayers and support of Justapaz, the peace and justice ministry of the Colombia Mennonite Church, or by visiting Colombia on accompaniment delegations with the Mennonite Central Committee and Witness for Peace, North Americans can work to show God's steadfast love.

Clarence Jordan suggests that "God's movement" is a better contemporary translation than "the reign of God." Through his parables and sermons about God's reign, Jesus calls us to participate in building a world that embodies God's justice, as the Lord's Prayer says, on earth and in heaven. In his first words in Mark's Gospel, Jesus announces that the kingdom of God is near and challenges his hearers to repent and believe the Good News. In the parallel passage in Luke 4:18, Jesus describes more "reign of God" actions: good news to the poor, release of captives, freedom for the oppressed—all reflecting the delivering love of the Jesus Christ we follow and imitate.

Children's Time

Materials: A picture of a rainbow and a picture of a model of Noah's ark

Who knows what this is a picture of? When do you see a rainbow? What is special about a rainbow? What colors do you see in a rainbow? Our Bible story today is about the time when God gave the rainbow to people. Who knows who Noah was? Noah and his family listened to God and built a big boat and found all kinds of animals to stay on the boat while there was a big flood. After the water dried up and Noah and Noah's family and the animals got off the boat, God talked with Noah. God made a promise to every living creature that was on Noah's ark—Noah and Noah's family and birds and every animal. God promised Noah that there would never again be a big flood and that God was giving them a rainbow to remind them of that promise. The rainbow was a reminder that God would take care of them.

So when you see a rainbow, remember that God takes care of you. God helps us take care of other people. You might pick up something that an elderly person dropped on the floor, or you might make cookies for homeless children at a shelter. You can care for people who are hungry by keeping a piggy bank and putting your pennies in it, then giving it to your church for a hunger offering.

Musical Suggestions

O God, Our Help in Ages Past—BP 123

A Part of Me Lives in Africa (A World that Hungers)—BP 196

Break Not the Circle of Enabling Love—BP 145

Michelle Tooley

Second Sunday of Lent

RCL: Genesis 17:1-7, 15-16; Psalm 22:23-31; Romans 4:13-25;
   Mark 8:31-38

LM: Genesis 22:1-2, 9a, 10-13, 15-18; Psalm 116:10, 15, 16-17, 18-19;
   Romans 8:31b-34; Mark 9:2-10

Good news seems sweetest to those who suffer, who are in the midst of what St. John of the Cross calls "the dark night of the soul." In Psalm 22, David, like many who suffer, feels that God has rejected and abandoned him. Physical signs accompany his misery: he is so emaciated that he can count his bones, so thirsty that he has a dry mouth, so destitute that others are dividing his clothes, so weak that evildoers may destroy him. The millions of people who live daily in hunger and poverty often experience David's physical symptoms of misery.

With God's apparent silence in the midst of his suffering, David's sense of isolation and hopelessness grows. Today's psalm verses follow David's despair and his urgent cry for deliverance. Recalling that in the past God heard his cries and delivered him, David recovers his sense of hope in God and resolves to act faithfully. David's personal memory of God's attentiveness to his needs reminds us of God's response to Moses in Exodus 3:7: "I have observed the misery of my people who are in Egypt; I have heard their cry on account of their taskmasters. Indeed, I know their sufferings, and I have come down to deliver them." What good news to individuals like David! What good news to the family that lives in an abandoned school bus in the Mississippi Delta! What good news to Sudanese refugees who have walked for days looking for food and shelter! What good news to the 1.2 billion people who live on less than one dollar a day! God hears the cries of suffering people, sees their pain, and acts to deliver them.

David goes on to reflect that "the poor shall eat and be satisfied" (Ps 22:26), which is either a statement of God's intentions for poor people or David's plan for action. Regardless of whether David intends his words as a promise of his personal action or a sign of the reign of God, he clearly identifies poor people as the afflicted ones to whom God responds and to whom individuals should respond. In the United States some people think of two categories of poverty: the deserving poor and the undeserving poor. The undeserving poor are considered lazy, shiftless people who have caused their own poverty. Notice that the biblical writer makes no such distinction but speaks inclusively of any persons who are poor.

Archbishop Oscar Romero referred to the poor in the Bible and in El Salvador as *los empobrecidos* (those made poor), not *los pobres* (the poor), pointing to the systemic connections that create and exacerbate poverty. May we live in the world with the courage to ask why people are poor and how we have been complicit in their poverty. May we use our time and talents designing and implementing policies and programs to end poverty, rather than discussing which poor person deserves food. May we live in a world where those who are poor will eat and be satisfied!

In the gospel reading from Mark 8, after teaching that the Son of Man would suffer, be rejected, killed, and rise again, Jesus advises all who would follow him to deny themselves, take up their cross, and follow him. In El Salvador in the 1980s, Archbishop Romero understood the implications of Jesus' call to "take up the cross," a response that led to his assassination. For Romero, Gospel faithfulness translated into a life standing in solidarity with the poor.[1]

Children's Time

1. Talk about when the children feel bad and when bad things seem to keep happening to them. Some might have gotten involved in a

1. For more on Archbishop Romero's life, see the reflection for the Fifth Sunday of Lent, pp. 74–75. See also Marie Dennis, Renny Golden, and Scott Wright, *Oscar Romero: Reflections on His Life and Writings* (Maryknoll, N.Y.: Orbis Books, 2000).

series of fights or disagreements or done badly on several school assignments, and their parents and teachers seem disappointed with them. Talk about how they feel and what they can do about it: pray and ask God for help, talk with their parents or teachers, or talk with a friend. Discuss how in those situations it helps to remember other tough times and what helped to resolve the problems in those cases.

2. Ask children what their favorite meal is and what it feels like to have just finished it. Show pictures of poor children, and ask what their favorite meal might be. Read Psalm 22:26 to the children and talk about how God wants hungry children to "eat and be satisfied." Ask children how their family can help; then talk about ways your church helps meet hunger needs in your town and throughout the world.

Musical Suggestions

When the Poor Ones (Cuando el Pobre)—BP 154

The Lord Hears the Cry of the Poor—BP 109

You Shall Cross the Barren Desert (Be Not Afraid)—BP 208

Michelle Tooley

Third Sunday of Lent

RCL: Exodus 20:1-17; Psalm 19; 1 Corinthians 1:18-25; John 2:13-22
LM: Exodus 20:1-17 or 20:1-3, 7-8, 12-17; Psalm 19:8, 9, 10, 11;
  1 Corinthians 1:22-25; John 2:13-25; or the readings from Year A
  (see first volume, p. 67) may be used

On my tenth birthday, when I received my first allowance, my father
had the "money talk" with me. He explained about tithing and how we
are God's partners in the world. Years later, as a new college student,
my father gave me the second part of that talk—advice about how my
values and my money are connected. He said, "Remember that your
checkbook faithfully records what your values and beliefs are."

Two of today's texts address our economic priorities, what we do
with the "things" of our lives (including our money) and where our
primary allegiance lies. The gospel reading offers a negative example:
what *not* to do with a place of worship and what not to participate in,
while several of the Ten Commandments have economic relevance.

The gospel passage comes immediately after Jesus changes the water
into wine at the wedding party in Cana. Jesus travels to Jerusalem for
Passover, where he discovers a bustle of activity in the Temple, not
with prayers, fasts, or discussion of texts, but with commercial activities that cheapen the Temple's purpose. After driving out the merchants,
Jesus denounces their practices because they have turned God's house
into a shopping mall.

If Jesus were in the United States today, what would he be cleansing
from our temples, from our churches and chapels and cathedrals? What

would Jesus say about the food courts in some large churches? How would he address the workers at the McDonald's in the church in Houston? Would he be horrified or pleased by the huge amounts spent every year for building and renovation of church facilities? What words would he say to congregations that charge money for recreation facilities or refuse entrance to anyone but church members? Visiting our churches and religious organizations, would he denounce our marketing activities and examine our budgets for economic priorities in the same way that he scrutinized the misplaced priorities of the Temple that day?

There are churches throughout the United States and in the global South that offer positive examples of how to avoid the trap of consumerism and cultural captivity. Several years ago members of Edgehill United Methodist Church in Nashville, Tennessee, known for their work with poor and homeless people, gathered with an outside facilitator to see if the spending decisions in their church budget reflected what they believed about the church's mission. This exercise would be helpful for every individual and every church because the desires we embrace and express often are not reflected in our economic decisions.

At least three of the Ten Commandments offer economic guidance as we ask to whom we profess allegiance. The commandment to have no other gods before or against the Lord our God is timely in a country that in recent years has been rocked by corporate scandals, and where the profit-makers often are members of Christian churches. The obvious question resounds: Who is your God and whom do you serve? If you are the CEO of a corporation, is your primary loyalty to your God, your board of directors, your shareholders, or your employees? In a culture in which the domination of money is a plague, all of us— rich and poor, business owner and employee, homeowner and homeless—are tempted by other gods and must consider our loyalties. Do we express our loyalties in a way that honors faith life, family life, and work life?

The eighth commandment assumes the implicit right to private and community property, and pronounces the obvious lesson not to steal. Before we pat ourselves on the back for not robbing anyone this week, perhaps we ought to delve deeper. Along with other homeowners, I profit on my taxes from what I pay in interest on my mortgage. Am I a thief if I don't advocate for comparable tax savings for those without homes, who are usually poor people? Am I living ethically when I support politicians who craft laws only in favor of those who are wealthy while millions go hungry, or when I buy clothing produced in factories where the workers have been paid unfair wages? Am I stealing when the richest one-fifth of the world's population (which includes my country) uses up 86 percent of the world's resources, while the poorest fifth only consumes 1 percent?[1]

The tenth commandment, "Do not covet," is closely related to the eighth commandment. In Joshua 7, Achan is punished for coveting the spoil from Jericho, then stealing it. George Pixley, Old Testament professor at the Seminario Bautista in Managua, Nicaragua, suggests that this law may be particularly targeted toward those with power who use their privilege to take what belongs to their weaker neighbor.[2] When we look at our society today, coveting manifests itself in the insatiable hunger for material possessions. The Bible continues to offer sound, real-life advice about economic activity for Christians and churches.

Children's Time

Materials: Katherine Scholes' *Peace Begins with You*

One of our Bible readings today is from 1 Corinthians, one of Paul's letters to a church in Corinth. The people in this church had problems getting along with one another. They had different ideas and quarreled and didn't work together. They even had problems with Communion. Some church members would get there early and eat everything, and then when other hungry members arrived, there wasn't any food or drink. Clearly, they didn't know how to be peacemakers. In many countries in the world people are hungry because their countries are at war. Sometimes the country is spending a lot of money on guns and bombs, and it doesn't have money for the poor. At other times war destroys the crops that are the food supply, or people have to leave their homes and become refugees. Our missionaries may be in lands with wars, and they help with giving food. You can help by learning to be a peacemaker. You can pray for peace and work for a world that is more peaceful. Read parts of Katherine Scholes' *Peace Begins with You* , especially "How to Be a Peacemaker."

> But first of all, learn about yourself, about why you think, believe, feel, and act as you do. Learn how to listen and how to see things

1. United Nations Development Program, 1999.
2. George Pixley, *On Exodus* (Maryknoll, N.Y.: Orbis Books, 1987) 139.

from another point of view. Learn how to solve problems peacefully in your own life, because peace begins with you—in your own backyard.[3]

Musical Suggestions

The Lord Hears the Cry of the Poor—BP 109

When Israel Was in Egypt's Land (Go Down Moses)—BP 164

We Are Called to Be Peacemakers—BP 97

In Christ There Is No East or West—BP 87

3. Katherine Scholes, *Peace Begins with You* (Boston: Sierra Club Books/Little, Brown and Company, 1989) 36.

Michelle Tooley

◼

Fourth Sunday of Lent

◼

RCL: Numbers 21:4-9; Psalm 107:1-3, 17-22; Ephesians 2:1-10; John 3:14-21

LM: 2 Chronicles 36:14-16, 19-23; Psalm 137:1-2, 3, 4-5, 6; Ephesians 2:4-10; John 3:14-21

The Bible offers guidelines for God's economy, with special concern for poor and vulnerable members of society. Those guidelines make provision for poor people through gleaning laws and special treatment for widows, orphans, and strangers, while the Jubilee tradition provides rest for people, land, and animals and fresh beginnings for slaves and debtors.

The Roman Catholic reading from 2 Chronicles draws wisdom about the sabbatical year from the Jubilee tradition. Every seventh year debts are canceled, slaves are freed, and land and people rest from their labor and trust God to provide for their physical needs. Chronicles echoes Jeremiah's prophecy that God judges Judah because they have not kept the sabbatical year. Even after repeated warnings from Jeremiah and other prophets, the citizens of Judah make fun of the prophets and ignore God's laws. The text asserts that because of their refusal to practice personal and corporate morality, God allows the Babylonians to defeat the Israelites and take them into slavery. Soon they would find themselves in exile, unable to sing the songs of Zion (Ps 137:3-4).

In a political science classroom in the United Kingdom more than a decade ago, students gave the world a reason to sing. The professor and African students discussed the biblical Jubilee texts in light of the

71

seriousness of what UNICEF called the biggest killer of children in the Third World—the external debt of the world's poorest countries. Thousands of Christians dared to ask what the Jubilee texts might look like in our world today. From their conversations and study grew a worldwide, faith-based movement of grassroots activism that changed the programs and priorities of the world's richest countries and the international financial institutions. The Jubilee 2000 movement, with groups in countries throughout the world, dares to work for the cancellation of debt of the world's poorest countries in ways that help poor people. In the United States, the Jubilee 2000/U.S.A. coalition won a substantial victory in Congress after months of telephone calls, visits, and letters to members of Congress. Debt remains a staggering problem for the world's poorest countries, but the victory in Congress represents a strong first step.

Psalm 137 takes place while the Hebrew people are in exile in Babylon. As they mourn the difficulty of singing God's song in a strange land, they remember Jerusalem and the life they discarded because of their unfaithfulness to God. Like those exiles, we too are exiles called to sing God's song in a strange land. Like those children of God, we are called to repentance and remembrance. God invites us to cry out in repentance for our complicity with the powers and authorities of the world even as we announce God's message of justice and compassion for all God's children. The Lenten season offers time for reflection on our personal and corporate morality, and opportunities to advocate for poor people. To whom can we sing? To Congress, our state legislators, local officials, the World Bank, the International Monetary Fund, to our denominations and local churches.

Singing God's song begins and ends with God's gratuitous love in the familiar words of John 3:16. Sabbath living grows from God's creation of a world with abundance, a world with *shalom*. Because God loves the world, disciples should practice and preach God's love, an inclusive love for all creation and for the whole person. Quite practically, love translates into ensuring that basic human needs like food, water, and shelter are provided for everyone. As we sing God's song in this strange land, may we dare to work toward God's economy, which values all God's creation.

Children's Time

Materials: A globe and *A Country Far Away*

How do you know that your family loves you? When I was a little girl, my mother would make special food for me on ordinary days. She would come home from work and make my favorite cookies—oatmeal raisin cookies—or she would bake an apple just for me. When I had a stomach ache, she would bring me her favorite comforter, made of soft, pink material, for me to hold. What kinds of things do your mom or dad do to let you know that they love you?

One of today's Scripture readings tells us what God did for us to show us God's special love. John 3:16 says that God loved the world so much that God sent Jesus to the world. Often we read the verse as being just about Jesus, but this verse also tells us that God loves every single person in the world, which means that every person in the world has something very important in common— God loves us in a special way.

Today we're going to read a book about how we live and how some other special people in Africa live.[1] Before reading the book, show children where Africa is, and point out that it has many different countries. Read the story and then ask the children what differences they see between the children in the United States and Africa. Tell them that many children and adults in Africa are poor and hungry, but there are also many Africans who are working to end hunger. As Christians, we can love other people around the world, and we can begin by learning about people in other countries. We can show our love by doing special things for children and adults in other countries. How can we love people in Africa?

Musical Suggestions

My Life Flows On in Endless Song (How Can I Keep from Singing?) —BP 125

Sing Justice to the Wilderness—BP 187

Jesu, Jesu, Fill Us with Your Love—BP 218

Live into Hope of Captives Freed—BP 217

1. Nigel Gray, *A Country Far Away* (New York: Orchard Books, 1988). This is a picture book that compares the lives of children in a United States city with those in an African village.

Michelle Tooley

Fifth Sunday of Lent

RCL: Jeremiah 31:31-34; Psalm 51:1-12 or Psalm 119:9-16;
   Hebrews 5:5-10; John 12:20-33

LM: Jeremiah 31:31-34; Psalm 51:3-4, 12-13, 14-15; Hebrews 5:7-9;
   John 12:20-33

As we proceed toward Jesus' passion in John's Gospel, we move increasingly toward the cross, encountering Jesus' words about his death and the cost of discipleship. Responding to a question about some Greeks who want to visit him, Jesus tells Philip and Andrew that a "grain of wheat falls into the earth and dies . . . [to] bear much fruit. Those who love their life lose it . . . Whoever serves me must follow me" (12:24-26).

Formerly a quiet parish priest and academic, Oscar Romero discovered the cost of discipleship and the danger of following Jesus during his three years as archbishop in El Salvador, ending when he was assassinated while celebrating the Eucharist on March 24, 1980. Shortly after he was named archbishop, Romero was transformed by the impoverished people in his beloved El Salvador and spent his brief remaining ministry speaking out boldly on behalf of oppressed people in a war-torn land. Like Dietrich Bonhoeffer, Romero acknowledged the Gospel's historical demands and the sin of staying silent and uninvolved. For him, this meant denouncing an economic systemic that enriched the few and impoverished the majority of Salvadorans. He criticized the torture and murder of thousands of poor people and stood with them in their suffering. More than anything, Romero called the Church to solidarity with those on the margins.

What a terrible thing to have lived quite comfortably, with no suffering, not getting involved in problems, quite tranquil, quite settled, with good connections politically, economically, socially—lacking nothing, having everything. To what good? They will lose their lives. "But those who for love of me [Jesus] uproot themselves and accompany the people and go with the poor in their suffering and become incarnated and feel as their own the pain and the abuse—they will secure their lives, because my Father will reward them."[1]

God's call echoes again in Psalm 51, associated with David's words of repentance after Nathan confronts him following his violation of Bathsheba. Aware of his sins, David speaks of a fresh beginning and promises to teach others God's ways. Who confronts and teaches national leaders today as the prophet Nathan confronted David? With a political system and a national election structure dominated by big money, U.S. citizens often assume that paid lobbyists and professional politicians and their staff know what is best. Have we misunderstood patriotism as uncritical loyalty to our nation? We forget that we follow a powerful God who calls our nation to minister to the least, as Jesus says in Matthew 25. God calls us to act as Nathan did, confronting our government with the sins in our structures and systems, acting in concert with those whom our policies have left out, overlooked, or forgotten.

Like David, we have the opportunity to teach others God's ways of liberation and justice. How appropriate during the Lenten season that we examine the sin in our lives as well as in the structures and systems of our society—and that we use our citizenship to confront leaders and call them to changed behaviors. Bread for the World uses advocacy to call Congress to changed behavior for poor and oppressed people in the United States and the world.

Children's Time

Materials: Six crayons and two dollars

In Jesus' world, roads were dusty and people walked a lot, so their feet were often tired and dirty. In our gospel passage today one of

1. From a homily on Jeremiah 31:31-34, Hebrews 5:7-9, John 12:20-33 on April 1, 1979. Oscar Romero, *The Violence of Love* (Farmington, Pa.: Plough Publishing House, 1998) 127–28.

Jesus' best friends, Mary, cleans his feet and rubs them with lotion, a loving, thoughtful action. Probably Mary had walked often in her sandals and remembered what it felt like to be tired. Mary knew Jesus well, and she wanted to be kind and helpful to him.

In our world today there are a lot of people. Do you know how many? Put down six crayons and have the children count the crayons together. Are there six people? No, there are six billion, which is a lot of people. Count again, one billion to six billion.

Do you know how much two dollars will buy? Will it buy a Happy Meal? What if you had only two dollars for one day, for all your food? Pick up three crayons and tell them that this many people live on two dollars each day, and most of them don't have enough food to eat. How can we be kind and helpful to the three billion people who live on two dollars a day? We can pray for them and work with our church on projects to collect money or supplies for them. We can also write letters or draw pictures and send them to our President and Congress to tell them that we want our nation to help all the hungry people in the world. Just as Mary was kind to Jesus, we want to be kind to people who are hungry.

Musical Suggestions

Lord God, Your Love Has Called Us Here—BP 108

Jesu, Jesu, Fill Us with Your Love—BP 218

Lift Ev'ry Voice and Sing—BP 177

I Have Decided to Follow Jesus—BH 305

Never the Blade Shall Rise—GC 706

Michelle Tooley

◧

Passion Sunday/Palm Sunday

◧

Liturgy of the Palms

RCL: Mark 11:1-11 or John 12:12-16; Psalm 118:1-2, 19-29

LM: Mark 11:1-10 or John 12:12-16

Liturgy of the Passion

RCL: Isaiah 50:4-9a; Psalm 31:9-16; Philippians 2:5-11;
    Mark 14:1–15:47 or Mark 15:1-39 (40-47)

LM: Isaiah 50:4-7; Psalm 22:8-9, 17-18, 19-20, 23-24;
    Philippians 2:6-11; Mark 14:1–15:47 or 15:1-39

On Palm Sunday 2002 my friend Cindy arrived in Jerusalem, where Jesus had entered nearly two thousand years earlier to the sounds of cheers and hosannas. For Jesus, underlying the sounds of welcome and jubilation were a city and state living under Roman occupation. In 2002 no one heard cheers and hosannas; in fact, fear and tension were almost palpable. Torn by violence, suicide bombings, and Israeli occupation of Palestinian areas, Jerusalem and the Holy Land are places of danger and tension. After a day in Jerusalem, Cindy traveled the few miles to Bethlehem, where she worked as a human rights observer in a refugee camp with Christian and Muslim Palestinians. There Cindy and other observers discovered and grieved at the human costs of war—the deaths of combatants and of innocent women, men, and children.

From a hunger perspective, the costs of war far exceed tombstones in a graveyard. During war, costs include increased hunger and poverty

77

because of disruption of the growth cycle for farmers and the destruction of food, whether in stores, markets, or fields. Land mines buried in fields limit planting and harvesting crops and cause death or dismemberment for farmers. Destruction of infrastructure, like bridges, roads, water sources, and electrical plants, translates into unsafe water supply and less access to food and healthcare. Social spending decreases as military spending increases, so less money is spent on development. Increased violence and instability may result in non-governmental organizations curtailing relief and development projects. Unemployment increases and city dwellers lose the means to make money to buy food. Knowing the economic consequences of war offers powerful incentives to reduce violence and build peace.

The lesson from Isaiah culminates in a call for solidarity in the midst of suffering. Solidarity means entering into the experience of other persons, knowing that we can never completely understand their reality, but caring enough to try to understand by putting our body in their place and accompanying them in their struggle.

Far away from her classrooms at Belmont University, another North American woman, Cheryl Glenn, discovered solidarity in Managua, Nicaragua, while studying Third World debt and its effect on Nicaragua's people. In one meeting Cheryl listened to union leaders tell how they had been fired that day from their jobs in the Free Trade Zone. The next morning Cheryl's group accompanied the fired union leaders to the factories in the Zone, as seventeen thousand other workers arrived for the day's labor. As they wove through the masses of workers, Cheryl's new friends pointed out workers looking out through barbed wire, muscled gang members hired to intimidate union members, guards with machine guns, and workers undergoing searches as they entered the factories. A translator explained the abysmal working conditions and poor salaries that the union was struggling to change, adding that only the week before, the union had staged a peaceful protest and a work slowdown with hundreds of workers participating. As Cheryl took photos, she noticed the fired union leaders were smiling, despite being unemployed in a country with staggering poverty. As the leaders walked with the group back to the gate of the Free Trade Zone, they hugged everyone and bade the foreigners farewell, making clear that the visit had met their hopes and expectations. The union leaders reentered the Free Trade Zone, committed anew to their struggle for just wages and better working conditions.

In Mark's Gospel an unnamed woman accompanies Jesus in his struggle by anointing his head with oil, thus teaching two interrelated lessons: the importance of extravagant love and generosity toward those who are poor. The woman invests in expensive perfume and, upon anointing Jesus' head, is the target of severe criticism from onlookers, since, after all, the money could have fed poor people. Jesus praises her action with a response that seems puzzling to those who know his concern for those on the margins. Some in our churches have used verse 7 to resignedly explain the inevitability of poverty and even justify a "lifeboat ethics" approach to helping poor people. But those who know the Hebrew Scriptures recognize a theme from the sabbatical year embedded in Jesus' apparently dismissive words. Jesus' words that there are always those in need among us echo Deuteronomy 15, which ends with words Jesus knew he needn't repeat for those around him: "I therefore command you, open your hand to the poor and needy neighbor in your land."

The psalmist's cry in Psalm 22, "I can count all my bones," evokes pictures of listless children with emaciated bodies in North Korea, Ethiopia, Sudan, and other parts of our world. These images are an ever-present reminder of the lessons in the anointing story. God wants all children to be loved extravagantly and for us to be generous to those who are poor and needy. Annual resources like the United Nations Development Program's *Human Development Report* and Bread for the World Institute's *Hunger Report* describe the shape of hunger in different countries of the world.

Children's Time

Materials: Palm branches

How many of you have ever seen a tree with this kind of leaves? Palm trees grow in countries or states that don't have snow. They grow in places like Florida and parts of California and in the country where Jesus grew up. Today is a special day at church because we remember Jesus coming into Jerusalem on a donkey. Now Jesus had been to Jerusalem before, but this time people saw him and knew that he was special. They waved the branches when he rode by, and they said "Hosanna" and other things, which meant how glad they were to see him. They were glad to see him because he was God's Son, something that makes us glad too. They welcomed him into Jerusalem.

What do you say when you see someone that you're glad to see? What do you do? Do you hug that person or shake her hand? Do you draw a special picture for him or give him special food? One way that we can show people that they are special is to treat them like they're special. We call this "hospitality," and it is good, not only for people we know but also for people we don't know. During the Christmas holidays some families serve food together at a soup kitchen, or they make dinner for homeless people who spend the night at their church.

Musical Suggestions

Bread of the World in Mercy Broken—BP 110, 111

In Remembrance—BH 365

Tell Me the Story of Jesus—BH 122

Christ Is the Truth, the Way—BP 179

Additional Resource

Many churches encourage parishioners to reflect on the passion of Jesus Christ using the Stations of the Cross. Each year the Religious Working Group on the World Bank and IMF publishes a book, *The Economic Way of the Cross,* for people of faith to reflect on Jesus' passion in light of the suffering of women, men, and children throughout the world. See www.sndden.org/rwg/cross.htm.

Michael Seifert and Ruben Becerra

Holy (Maundy) Thursday

RCL: Exodus 12:1-4 (5-10) 11-14; Psalm 116:1-2, 12-19;
  1 Corinthians 11:23-26; John 13:1-17, 31b-35
LM: Exodus 12:1-8, 11-14; Psalm 116:12-13, 15-16bc, 17-18;
  1 Corinthians 11:23-26; John 13:1-15

The three holiest days for Christians begin with a celebration of the Eucharist that includes an ancient act of housekeeping: the washing of feet. The three days will end with the proclamation of a gospel that speaks of yet more housekeeping: a visit to the tomb for the required cleaning of the corpse. In the person of Jesus the Christ, these housekeeping details take on an entirely different significance. For the Body of Christ, the Church, it is precisely these "details" that have become, for so many people, a matter of life and death.

We begin our celebration of the Easter Triduum with the command to wash feet, a part of the body so significant to the Jews, who became a people only after marching for forty years through the desert. The reading from Exodus recalls that fearsome night of the first Passover, when the Lord's mighty command to "set my people free" is then taken

81

seriously. The Lord orders the Israelites to eat, for eat they must if they are to survive this "passing over" from slavery to freedom.

The references to this first Passover in the gospel are clear. It is a celebration; it is Jesus' Passover meal, for it is his time to obey God's call to make the "passing over." He too must eat so that he can finish his journey. But first he offers a lesson—no, he gives a command. He bends down and begins to wash his friends' feet. Thus begins Holy Thursday. Thus begins our celebration of the Passover.

Each Holy Thursday, just outside of Brownsville, Texas, a group of ministers gather at what the U.S. Immigration and Naturalization Service calls a "processing center." This is a jail where our government locks up women and men who have illegally come to this country, most of them from south of the border, seeking the privilege of washing our feet, our laundry, our floors, our streets. The feet these ministers wash at this Holy Thursday celebration are quite different from most of the other feet that will be washed in church sanctuaries across the land. Here the ministers honor the torn feet of a woman who was caught when she got lost while roaming the thorny desert that lies just north of the Mexico-Texas border. In this jail a priest will carefully wash and dry the misshapen, hard-callused feet of an Indian from Guatemala, feet that have never found shoes to be a comfort. On this day, in anticipation of Easter, water and soap will run over tired feet, veined feet, bruised and bloodied feet. Poor people's feet. Feet not made for the kind of walking that they have had to do.

Washing feet on Holy Thursday is always a startling event. The baring of feet in the holiest of places, the splashing of water and the perfume of soap, the awkwardness of kneeling on the floor, and the almost painful intimacy of touching a stranger's feet are disquieting moments. Jesus himself manages to alarm his guests when he, the honored one, bends down to do the work of the house slave. His anxious friends demand, "Why are you doing this?" This question echoes that of the youngest child at the paschal feast ("Why do we do this?"), which in its own way is but an echo of questions from a much earlier moment of consternation, that of the first Passover from the anonymity of slavery to the dignity of a free people.

Foot-washing, in Jesus' time, was part of the ritual of welcoming, of recognizing, gratefully, the distance that someone had traveled to grace the family with a visit. In our day, of course, we celebrate this ritual only in church, and then only during the celebration of the Triduum (although some southern evangelical communities frequently celebrate foot-washing as part of their Eucharist). Much more common are the rites we have developed that celebrate "un-welcoming." Among many examples, these include the yearly celebration of outrageous amounts of money appropriated to the Border Patrol to keep out people whom we all secretly want to employ, the "gating" of our communities, and the creation of the Department of Homeland Security.

"Do this in memory of me." We are ordered to strip down, to kneel down, to wash and welcome the stranger. This gesture is what begins our own journeys to salvation: the welcoming of the stranger, the opening of the doors to our homes, to our communities, to our hearts.

Children's Time [MM]

Lead the children to the altar/communion table. Ask, "What is this?" Then ask, "What do we do here?" and "Who comes here to eat this meal?" Who comes? The Body of Christ—our sisters and brothers of this congregation/parish. Point out that this is like a family meal, where the family eats and drinks together. Remind them that God always provides enough for God's family to eat (even though there are only small portions at this holy table). Ask them to consider how important meals and eating are, that Jesus chose a meal to gather his people, saying, "Do *this* in remembrance of me." That's why it's appropriate to pray to God and remember Jesus every time we eat—at church, at home, at restaurants, wherever. It's also an excellent time to remind the children that God wants everyone to have enough to eat, that everyone should be able to eat every meal.

Musical Suggestions [LH]

Jesu, Jesu, Fill Us with Your Love—PH 367

Serving You—GC 410

We Gather in Worship—GC 750

Community of Christ—NCH 314

Now the Silence—CH 415

Michael Seifert and Ruben Becerra

Good Friday
===========

RCL: Isaiah 52:13–53:12; Psalm 22; Hebrews 10:16-25 or 4:14-16;
  5:7-9; John 18:1–19:42

LM: Isaiah 52:13–53:12; Psalm 31:2, 6, 12-13, 15-16, 17, 25;
  Hebrews 4:14-16; 5:7-9; John 18:1–19:42

Good Friday is senseless. Jesus' crucifixion destroys all theological categories, however elegant and carefully wrought they might be. While Calvary sits at the very center of Christian reflection, Jesus' death on the cross stuns even the deepest faith in an all-powerful, loving God. Indeed, the last words of the One who taught us to pray "Our Father" are words of despair. Yet this death inspires even those who had him executed (John 19:37). The theologies of God as the all-powerful, all-good One become secondary before the cry of this Poor Man.

On Calvary, all of the rote responses that we are taught (most notably "Jesus died to save me from my sins") are soon seen to be banal exercises in spiritual self-centeredness. Jesus did not die just because I sinned. He was executed because he valued the human being over and above religious faithfulness, allegiance to the political powers-that-be, and the status quo of the rich and famous. He was executed and died because all of us are sinful and because human systems and religions, legal processes and "safety nets" both then and now are sinful. In the Jerusalem of two thousand years ago and in present-day Palestine, in sub-Saharan Africa and in the state of Texas, we have managed to create entire ways of life that incline to succor the powerful and feed the already satiated. That the poor and weak suffer at the hands of governments is not surprising. That the Son of God did is another thing altogether.

Among Hispanic poor people, Good Friday is *the* holy day of the year. Not Easter, not Christmas, but Good Friday. During the midday heat people throng the streets and march for hours in silence behind a man portraying Jesus carrying a cross. Men dressed as soldiers complete the scene. Each time a soldier whips the fellow playing Jesus, people gasp and cry out. In some places the actor is actually nailed to a cross. There is often blood and always many tears. In the evening hundreds of the grieving faithful silently follow a statue of Mary, the surviving mother, throughout the city.

These scenes are played out through the year. Any Roman Catholic church worth its salt has a realistic, garishly painted crucified Jesus up in front, a Jesus that is lovingly reverenced, touched, and kissed. A very fine liturgist on a visit to the Texas-Mexico border offered his criticism that there were "far too many crucified Jesuses in Hispanic churches, and not enough resurrected Christs." To which a local United Farm Workers activist responded, "In our poor lives, we don't know much about resurrection. We know a whole lot about betrayal. We know a whole lot about the powerful crucifying some poor, good person."

As our churches gather today to hear this awful Word of God, perhaps we should pray that our people properly receive this Word. Perhaps we can pray that we learn to reject the cowardice that Pilate so thoroughly displays. Perhaps that Word can yield the fruits of justice at last—when we recognize the entire peoples that the wealthy nations of the world have placed on the cross of progress. Perhaps this Good Friday will represent a turning toward Easter morning, when we commit ourselves to begin taking people down from the crosses upon which we have nailed them.

This will require a confession of sins, an admission of guilt, and a firm purpose not to sin again. In practical terms, it means reading the labels on our clothing and understanding that our shoes made in Indonesia crucified some poor teenager. It means taking seriously the Gospel call to a simple life. It means perhaps a spring break, not to Florida beaches to get away from it all, but to a Mexican border church to stare crucifixion in the face. It means standing up in public and denouncing capital punishment—not only that which occurs in prisons, but those slow-motion executions that begin in statehouses and on Capitol Hill, when hardhearted laws place business interests above those of children. It means gazing upon the face of this disfigured One, and recognizing in him my brother, my son, my sister, my daughter, my neighbor.

Children's Time [MM]

Lead the children to the most prominent cross in the sanctuary, preferably a rough Lenten cross, if your congregation uses one. Ask them why Jesus was crucified. Help them to discover as many of the reasons as they can: fear and jealousy (of the Pharisees); injustice (on the part of Pilate and the Romans); hatred and cruelty (of the crowd); and sinfulness in general (of all humanity). Many of the ugly elements of life came together to cause the death of the dear Lord Jesus. But it is important to point the children toward the Resurrection on this mournful Good Friday. Remind them that God's love, hope, joy, and power ultimately overcome the worst that humanity can muster. Today Jesus dies because of all that's wrong with the world; on Sunday, Jesus will rise again because of all that's right with God.

Musical Suggestions [LH]

O God, My God—NCH 515

O Praise the Gracious Power—PH 471

The Lord Hears the Cry of the Poor—BP 109

Michael Seifert and Ruben Becerra

◼

Easter Vigil

◼

RCL: Genesis 1:1–2:4a; Psalm 136:1-9, 23-26; Genesis 7:1-5, 11-18;
   8:6-18; 9:8-13; Psalm 46; Genesis 22:1-18; Psalm 16; Exodus 14:10-31;
   15:20-21; Exodus 15:1b-13, 17-18; Isaiah 55:1-11; Isaiah 12:2-6;
   Proverbs 8:1-8, 19-21; 9:4b-6; Psalm 19; Ezekiel 36:24-28; Psalm 42
   and 43; Ezekiel 37:1-14; Psalm 143; Zephaniah 3:14-20; Psalm 98;
   Romans 6:3-11; Psalm 114; Mark 16:1-8

LM: Genesis 1:1–2:2 or 1:1, 26-31a; Psalm 104:1-2, 5-6, 10, 12, 13-14,
   24, 35 or Psalm 33:4-5, 6-7, 12-13, 20-22; Genesis 22:1-18 or 22:1-2,
   9a, 10-13, 15-18; Psalm 16:5, 8, 9-10, 11; Exodus 14:15–15:1;
   Exodus 15:1-2, 3-4, 5-6, 17-18; Isaiah 54:5-14; Psalm 30:2, 4, 5-6,
   11-12, 13; Isaiah 55:1-11; Isaiah 12:2-3, 4, 5-6; Baruch 3:9-15,
   32–4:4; Psalm 19:8, 9, 10, 11; Ezekiel 36:16-17a, 18-28; Psalm 42:3,
   5; 43:3, 4 *(when baptism is celebrated);* Isaiah 12:2-3, 4bcd, 5-6 or
   Psalm 51:12-13, 14-15, 18-19 *(when baptism is not celebrated);*
   Romans 6:3-11; Psalm 118:1-2, 16-17, 22-23; Mark 16:1-7

Out into the dark night of Easter Saturday rings a whole series of readings that proclaim the justice of a faithful God who turns things inside out—darkness to light, slaves to free people, sadness to joy, death to life. This is a loving God who powerfully takes the side of the Just One and those who would follow him.

The story of this most holy night has always been at risk of being reduced to a series of pious reflections that promise heaven to those who behave well. In some cases God's powerful "NO!" to the execution of Jesus the Just One has been reduced to an eternal life insurance package

87

for the well-bred and the polite. Worse, this singular saving act of God in Jesus has been mistakenly understood as divine permission to leave aside the hard fact of our responsibility for our lives and for the lives of others—and for the working of God's will in our lives. The rather convenient argument runs: "If God's love is greater than death, then I am sure that God will forgive my cowardice, my lust, my needs." In a most perverse way, Easter, the celebration of an executed man-made-saint, has been turned into a pleasant season of bunny rabbits and bright-colored outfits, of Easter egg hunts and nice choral arrangements. The forces of greed, of fear, of evil could not be more pleased at how our Easter joy has been cheapened.

How, then, might we truly be able to sing out "Alleluia" with the choirs of angels and saints? What do our church, our community, and I need to do to experience and celebrate God's most powerful act in Jesus?

The Latin American theologian Jon Sobrino suggests that we take a lesson from poor believers who, in spite of their own crucifixions, continue to contemplate the Resurrection.[1] That we learn, in other words, how to hold together in our hearts both the horror of the Crucifixion and the wonder of the Resurrection—those facts twinned forever in the person of Jesus of Nazareth.

Jesus was not executed because he was a good person. Jesus was executed because he was obedient to the Word of God—he indeed spoke truth to power. The authority of his truth as well as its content reached the core of a political power that had become quite good at reducing poor human beings to objects of production. Jesus' truth touched the heart of a religious system that had in place a tidy system of separation and control.

That such a man was executed at that time is not at all surprising. Jesus himself expected it to be so. The surprise, of course, comes afterward, when God reaches down into the pit of death where this man has been cast and draws him out. The tomb of despair becomes a place of hope; the women who come to pay their last respects are sent forth with new News.

The gospel for this evening ends in a strange way: "They said nothing to anyone, for they were afraid" (Mark 16:8). A challenge, perhaps—or a call to faith. What shall *we* say of all that we have seen and

1. Jon Sobrino, *The Principle of Mercy: Taking the Crucified People from the Cross* (Maryknoll, N.Y.: Orbis Books, 1994).

heard? Dare we stand in the shadow of the cross, beneath the threat of humiliation, arrest, torture, or death and speak truth to power? Shall those of us gifted with the power to read, to think, to write—to proclaim —speak up on behalf of the billion poor people condemned to crucifixion, or shall we bite our tongues, saying nothing to anyone because of our fear? Shall we paint Easter eggs or create a new world order? Shall we enjoy Easter cake—or break the bread of the Eucharist?

Children's Time [MM]

Put on your best storytelling mindset! Explain to the children that the Vigil readings are part of the most important story in the history of the world—the story of God's people and of God's salvation for us. Tell (very briefly!) of the accursed slavery in Egypt and how God miraculously saved Israel. Tell how God kept Shadrach, Meshach, and Abednego from harm and how the prophets helped save the people by reminding them of God's call to feed hungry people and to care for all in need. Finally, tell of Jesus, he who was dead, now rising to life. Just tell the story! Help them to see that the Bible is one story, reaching this dramatic crescendo tonight. The final chapter—the denouement— is the process of making "(God's) will be done, on earth as in heaven." Help them see that with the power and help of the risen Jesus, the Church's work is to help finish the story.

Musical Suggestions [LH]

Christ Is Alive!—PH 108

Lord, Whose Love in Humble Service—GC 681

Christ Is Risen! Shout Hosanna!—GC 431

George S Johnson

Easter Sunday

RCL: Acts 10:34-43 or Isaiah 25:6-9; Psalm 118:1-2, 14-24;
1 Corinthians 15:1-11 or Acts 10:34-43; John 20:1-18 or Mark 16:1-8

LM: Acts 10:34a, 37-43; Psalm 118:1-2, 16-17, 22-23; Colossians 3:1-4
or 1 Corinthians 5:6b-8; John 20:1-9

Change is never easy. Mark Twain once said that "the only person who likes change is a wet baby." But change is necessary, perpetual, and a sign of growth. Without openness to change, decay sets in and death lurks in the shadows. Martin Luther said that the Word of God, whenever it comes, comes to change and renew the world.

Change is a dominant theme in the story of Peter and Cornelius in Acts 10. Peter's theology, including his attitude toward Gentiles, is transformed from exclusion to active fellowship. This is a good Sunday to talk about our own openness to change, especially that needed to respond to the suffering of hungry and poor people and damage to the environment. What needs to change in our worldview, in our relationship to nature, and in our attitudes toward those who are excluded?

The Peter/Cornelius encounter sets the stage for a strong word not only about the need for change but also about how difficult change can be when we think we have Scripture to support us in our traditional way of seeing things.

Peter's experience in Acts 10 is post-Easter and post-Pentecost. He has already experienced God's hand upon him through the healing experience in Acts 3. But despite his impressive résumé, Peter needs to get shaken before he is willing to change. Likewise for us, no matter

90

how many conversions we've had, we must be open to new insights. Our previous spiritual experiences are valuable, but they do not preclude the need for growth.

Peter's change comes through a face-to-face encounter with Cornelius, not through academic training or an inspirational sermon. In Acts we see that the Church's understanding of God's leading and God's presence grows out of the experience of being God's people. Pentecost is an experience before it is a doctrine. Most people who are changed in their understanding of, and compassion for, poor people tell of an experience involving a face-to-face encounter—at a homeless shelter or a soup kitchen, visiting a barrio, or taking part in a mission trip. This is a good Sunday to lift up the importance of being with, listening to, and feeling the pain of others through face-to-face experiences. (Give a personal example of how your attitude toward poverty has been changed in this way, or invite a lay person to testify to such an experience.)

For Peter to say that God shows no partiality and that all who fear God and do what is right are acceptable to God is a radical departure from previous understanding of the Torah, the Scriptures. Peter was well schooled in the traditions of his religious tradition—after all, he studied under Jesus himself. Peter was convinced that he was right in his attitude toward the Gentiles because it was from God—or so he thought. God had already blessed his ministry, which only strengthened his convictions. Still, Peter needed to change his thinking about boundaries and about the scope of God's compassion.

Could it be that we, too, need to rethink our interpretations of the Bible that may have influenced our response to hunger and poverty? Are we sometimes locked in rooms of theological safety? Third World theologians say that Christians in the privileged world need a conversion, a turning around, if they are ever to understand the biblical notion of oppression and justice. Change like that gives us fresh eyes to read the Bible. In my youth I was taught that the sin of Sodom was sexual; now I read in Ezekiel 16:49 that their sin also involved having surplus food while neglecting those who were poor.

Today's text from Acts includes some key words that relate to the Church's concern for justice for hungry people.

Peace (10:36). Jesus' message was peace *(shalom)*, which means wholeness, healing, abundant life for all God's creation. Pope Paul VI said, "If you want peace, work for justice." What did he mean? What change in our thinking would this imply for many of us?

Oppressed (10:38). Jesus was sent to minister to all who were oppressed (Luke 4:18). Elsa Tamez, in her book *Bible of the Oppressed*,[1] reminds us that oppression is the main cause of poverty in the Scriptures. Oppression is often a corporate action committed in the name of progress, profit, and national security. It is not really difficult to let others be greedy and oppressive on our behalf as long as we don't know about it. How can the sin of oppression be confessed in our Sunday liturgies and in our pastoral prayers? Another good reference is Thomas Hanks's *God So Loved the Third World*.[2]

Children's Time

Ask the children if they have ever changed their minds about something or if their parents have. Give an example of how you have changed your mind because of new evidence or a new experience. I used to think that girls were to be avoided, teased, or kept away from us boys. But I changed my mind. I am glad of that because now I have a wonderful wife and beautiful children, and I now think that girls are a gift from God. Sometimes we need to change our minds about certain people or certain things in order for us to show love to all people. In today's Bible reading from the Acts of the Apostles, God shows Peter how he needs to change his mind so that he can love all people. Can you think of an attitude that may keep us from loving certain people or from sharing with hungry people?

Musical Suggestions [LH]

At the Font We Start Our Journey—NCH 308

In the Bulb There Is a Flower—NCH 433

Christ Is Risen—UMH 307

Change Our Hearts—GC 394

In Christ There Is No East or West—PH 439, 440

---

1. Elsa Tamez, *Bible of the Oppressed* (Maryknoll, N.Y.: Orbis Books, 1982).
2. Thomas Hanks, *God So Loved the Third World: The Biblical Vocabulary of Oppression* (Maryknoll, N.Y.: Orbis Books, 1983).

George S Johnson

Second Sunday of Easter

RCL: Acts 4:32-35; Psalm 133; 1 John 1:1–2:2; John 20:19-31

LM: Acts 4:32-35; Psalm 118:2-4, 13-15, 22-24, 1 John 5:1-6;
    John 20:19-31

The Christian faith has profound economic implications. Any preaching of the Good News that shuns this reality denies the Gospel and Jesus' teachings. In Acts we see that one of the strong witnesses to Jesus' resurrection is the way his disciples order their economic lives. Resurrection and economics have spiritual connections to how the Church lives out its mission and are key to the Church's involvement in peace and justice ministry.

Acts 4 is about resurrection power in our living and our economics. Resurrection in Acts is not so much a doctrine to be believed as a power to be experienced. Trying to prove the historicity of the Resurrection may distract us from discovering this power in our lives as we engage the powers of domination today. The early Church community lived out this resurrection power in the way they arranged their lives, their relationships to one another, and their economics. The Church today needs to experience this kind of resurrection power if we are going to be an effective presence in a world torn apart by violence, poverty, greed, and fear.

One of the first important signs of resurrection power in the early Church was the strong sense of community. Verse 32 says the believers were of "one heart and soul." As you develop this text, explore what this would mean for your community. It goes back to creation, to the image of God, to the call to Israel, to the worship life of God's people, and to Jesus' teachings. This sense of community (family) meant that when one was in need of food, others would help meet that need.

Individualism is a cancer that has crept into our society and destroyed our need for one another, says Robert Bellah in *Habits of the Heart.*[1] The division between the haves and have-nots is partly due to this rampant individualism that is not balanced with community and love for neighbor. Where did Jesus' followers in the book of Acts learn this commitment to community? Was it not from Jesus' teachings, from their training in discipleship? Explore some of the elements in today's society that we need to resist if we are to be of one heart and one soul. Refer to the beautiful images of community in Psalm 133. Acts 2:42 says they "devoted" themselves to fellowship. An African saying says, "I can't be me without you."

Opportunities for humans to connect in small groups is an essential part of community life worldwide. Told that most North American women pipe water into their homes, a Nigerian woman grew somber. "How do the women speak to one another? If I didn't talk with the women at the village well, I wouldn't know about their lives," she said. Building small communities of faith is one of the major needs of the Church today, says Arthur Baranowski in his book *Creating Small Faith Communities.*[2] Social scientist Robert Wuthnow of Princeton University says the small group movement is the biggest social revolution of our times.

Because the Church has avoided bringing economics into the preaching of the Gospel, many in the family of God ignore the needs of poor and hungry people. We have fostered a kind of charity mentality that is void of justice. Jesus' resurrection enabled the disciples to practice their economics differently. It changed the way they viewed private ownership, sharing, and possessions, and made them more sensitive to inequalities among people. It gave them courage to resist the powers of domination.

Among the dominating powers in our contemporary society is greed. "Greed," says Jim Childs, "has a demeaning effect on everything from the quality of personal relationships to the just distribution of goods

---

1. Robert Bellah and others, *Habits of the Heart: Individualism and Commitment in American Life* (Berkeley: University of California Press, 1996).
2. Arthur Baranowski, *Creating Small Faith Communities* (Cincinnati: St. Anthony Messenger Press, 1988).

and the future of the environment."[3] The Christian ethic of compassion builds a caring community that seeks to overcome the often subtle allure of greed and counters the tendency for us to let our economic systems be greedy for us.

Living in community always leads outward to discern our place in the global community. These days people need to be introduced to the concept of globalization and its impact on people who are poor. Cynthia Moe-Lobeda has written a well-researched book about the effects of globalization on those who are poor.[4] She says that nearly every aspect of our lives is embedded in economic arrangements that destroy human beings and earth's life-systems, and she calls for resisting, revisioning, and rebuilding. Many people have no say in the global economic rules that affect their livelihoods, as wealthy people and structures set the rules of trade to favor those who are privileged.

Our lifestyles involve choices. Living consciously in community, both small and global, is not easy, but it is a vital part of our lives of faith.

Children's Time

To address the idea of community, have fun talking about the human body—how our bodies are made to function in harmony. Show what happens when one part of the body wants to be on its own. Pretend to take the thumb and separate it from the body, and place it all alone on the floor. Tell the thumb to be a thumb. "Thumb, do your thing." See, it cannot do anything without being attached to the body. Use this to talk about how we need each other and how our sisters and brothers in other parts of the world also need us and we them. Then tell how Christians in the book of Acts cared for each other. They were a community, a family. Distribute an insert from your faith tradition's hunger program that pictures a child in need. Have them hang the picture in their bedroom, where they will think about this part of their family and pray for them.

Musical Suggestions [LH]

All Who Hunger—FWS 2126

3. James Childs, Jr., *Greed: Economics and Ethics in Conflict* (Minneapolis: Fortress Press, 2000) v.
4. Cynthia Moe-Lobeda, *Healing a Broken World: Globalization and God* (Minneapolis: Fortress Press, 2002).

Draw Us in the Spirit's Tether—UMH 632

O God the Creator—NCH 291

Here in This Place—GC 839

O for a World—NCH 575

George S Johnson

Third Sunday of Easter

RCL: Acts 3:12-19; Psalm 4; 1 John 3:1-7; Luke 24:36b-48

LM: Acts 3:13-15, 17-19; Psalm 4:2, 4, 7-8, 9; 1 John 2:1-5a;
Luke 24:35-48

"Peace" is a word we often use to describe Jesus' ministry. The angel announcing Jesus' birth said that he came to bring peace on earth. Peace is often part of our worship liturgy, hymns, and prayers. In fact, we use the word so much that we may have lost its full meaning. Peace helps describe our responsibility toward poor and hungry people. Chapter 7 of Walter Brueggemann's book *Peace*[1] reminds us that peace is both a gift and a task.

In the text from Luke, the first message Jesus gives his disciples is one of peace. What did the disciples hear in the word "peace"? What did their hearts hear? Then what do we hear when we hear the word "peace"? What should we hear?

The most common Hebrew concept that relates to our word "peace" is *shalom,* meaning wellness, wholeness, healing . . . even salvation. The Lord wants *shalom* for those who are broken, hopeless, or filled

---

1. Walter Brueggemann, *Peace* (St. Louis: Chalice Press, 2001).

with fear. It has both a physical and spiritual dimension. If I want *shalom* for you, it means I am willing to share what I have so that you can have what you need. Your well-being is important to me. When Jesus said he came to give life abundant, he was talking about *shalom,* about peace. We need to be reminded that when we pray for peace in the world, we are saying that we are willing to share what we have so that the needs of others are met.

We cannot hear Jesus talk about peace without relating it to his life and death, the context of his Palestinian journey. Jesus lived under Roman occupation, which proclaimed *Pax Romana* ("Peace of Rome") as the gift of Roman rule in all the world. Jesus no doubt heard this slogan again and again. He knew this was propaganda, designed to obtain allegiance and obedience. The peace *(shalom)* he came to bring was an alternate kind of peace, one that did not depend on violence and domination. Jesus' peace did not leave out those who were poor, hungry, and oppressed. His disciples knew that Jesus was talking about something quite different than *Pax Romana,* involving a resistance to the illusory peace of military conquest.

Peace is connected to justice, to the right ordering of relationships. Peace as gift and task means that we will talk about the peace that passes understanding, the peace that calls us to share with others in need and work to end the oppression of those who don't count in today's market economy. Our concern for peace *(shalom)* encompasses the well-being of both individuals and society in pain, the pain of hunger and poverty.

Our advocacy work demonstrates that we want to bring peace to this world, to identify with those who are marginalized, and to give voice to the voiceless, as Jesus did. The call to be peacemakers is a call to resist the propaganda of *Pax Romana* still prevalent in the world. Our concern for peace will encompass the whole world, not just our country, our church, or our kind of people.

Jesus' appearance to the disciples leaves them startled and terrified, frightened and in doubt (Luke 24:37-38). These are emotions we understand; they often result from ignorance, lack of experience, or loss of perspective. Jesus reassures his disciples with his physical presence: "Touch me and see" (24:39). When we, too, are physically present with those who today are frightened by hunger, poverty, and injustice, we bring the divine presence to our neighbor and offer solidarity in the struggle for justice.

As Jesus opens his disciples' minds to understand the Scriptures (v. 45), we're reminded that church members must be challenged to use their minds and learn what it means to follow Jesus in today's ever-changing world. When our minds ignore what is happening to our neighbor, to our creation, to the least of these, we become indifferent to the actions we need to take. How many know that the United States, the world's wealthiest nation, is the only industrialized country that has failed to solve its domestic hunger problem? Do we know the implications of globalization for poor countries? Last week's reflection mentions this issue as well. Bread for the World Institute's *Hunger No More* materials can be very helpful in providing up-to-date information to people so that they can think about the reality of a world divided between the haves and have-nots. "Opening our minds" can be hard but rewarding work—an essential aspect of following the risen Christ.

Children's Time

Ask the children to give examples of when they've been afraid; listen to how they describe their fears. Tell about a time when you were afraid. Then ask them how they were helped, what took away their fear? Maybe it was someone's presence or touch, a story, or a song. Maybe it was more information or a willingness to risk. Tell about children today who are afraid for various reasons. Some children are afraid because they are hungry, and they don't know if there will be enough food for everyone in the family tomorrow. Some are afraid because they are sick, and they know they don't have any doctor to go to, no hospital, no medicine. Some children are afraid because their mother or father died yesterday from AIDS. We can help them not to be afraid by our gifts to the Hunger Appeal, by walking in the Hunger Walk, or by writing a letter to our nation's leaders. Show them a picture of a smiling child from another country, smiling because someone took their fears away.

Musical Suggestions [LH]

For One Great Peace—FWS 2185

Joy Dawned Again on Easter Day—NCH 241

Peace I Leave with You, My Friends—NCH 249

Lord of All Hopefulness—GC 578

George S Johnson

◼

Fourth Sunday of Easter

◼

RCL: Acts 4:5-12; Psalm 23; 1 John 3:16-24; John 10:11-18

LM: Acts 4:8-12; Psalm 118:1, 8-9, 21-23, 26, 28, 29; 1 John 3:1-2;
John 10:11-18

Many church members have heard a sermon on Jesus the Good Shepherd year after year without being challenged to change. The story is familiar, but we need a fresh approach that challenges us to love God and our neighbor with new energy. How does the Good Shepherd text, together with the lesson from 1 John, address a culture obsessed with security, profits, and revenge?

Moving from the obvious meaning of the metaphor of the shepherd (nurture and protection) to the meaning of laying down one's life can be risky. Western theology has emphasized so much Jesus' atonement for sin that we often miss the opportunity to talk honestly about 1 John 3:16-17. It is not only the Good Shepherd who lays down his life—we also are called to do this. Wow! "Who me? I'm not Jesus. My redemption is already paid for. I don't need to add to my salvation." And how do we lay down our lives, even if we want to? Isn't it enough to treasure in our hearts that Jesus laid down his life for us so that we can enjoy the still waters and green pastures?

And what does Psalm 23 mean: "He prepares a table before me in the presence of my enemies"? Could the shadow of death be those experiences in which we are called to lay down our lives for one another, especially those experiencing the shadows of death in their struggle to survive in the face of oppression?

There are few more provocative, disturbing, and soul-searching verses in Scripture than 1 John 3:17. It brings us right into the core of our faith with its economic implications. We have the world's goods. Our sisters and brothers are in need of food, in need of justice and opportunity. Neither the text from 1 John nor the Gospel passage allows us to spiritualize these references to love. Love is practical action on behalf of those in need.

It might be well to list some ways in which we have the world's goods and what we are doing with them. If we check our closets, our storage cabinets, our garages, our investment portfolios, our savings for the future, our trading power over less developed countries, we can better understand what John means by having the world's goods. Why are we so well off while others have so little, with millions living on less than two dollars a day? Check out *Hunger No More,* study material from Bread for the World Institute on domestic and international hunger, or the Catholic bishops' pastoral letter *Economic Justice for All,*[1] a look at Catholic teachings on social justice and the U.S. economy.

A missionary spoke at a church assembly that I attended. During a Bible study on the Rich Man and Lazarus in Luke 16, he asked the audience to please not get too upset when he said these words: "In many ways we in North America have gotten rich on the backs of the poor in the world." He knew that such talk is hard to hear because we are so used to thinking that our hard work, our free-market economy, our democratic values, and our freedoms have enabled us to become the wealthiest nation in the world. God has blessed us, and that is why we are prosperous. People need to hear the other side of the story. Example: Many Third World countries have to pay so much just on the interest they owe on their debts that there is little left to address poverty and education issues. Barbara Rumscheidt, describing the history of the debt crisis, says that countries in the global South have subsidized the North on a scale of 3 to 1.[2] When we talk about laying down one's life for our neighbors, it needs to be explained both individually and corporately. Good Shepherd love is about meeting the needs of other

1. *Economic Justice for All: Pastoral Letter on Catholic Social Teachings and the U.S. Economy* (Washington, D.C.: National Conference of Catholic Bishops, 1986).

2. Barbara Rumscheidt, *No Room for Grace: Economics and Ethics in Conflict* (Grand Rapids: Wm. B. Eerdmans, 1998) 148.

countries. This includes nations whose debts have them in bondage and nations where AIDS is killing up to 20 percent of the adult population. Remind people what happened when Sodom had the world's goods but neglected the poor (Ezek 16:49).

Dom Helder Camara, a Brazilian bishop, once said, "When I give food to the hungry they call me a saint. When I ask why are they hungry, they call me a communist." Getting beyond charitable responses to hunger and attacking its root causes are not easy and may mean getting our elbows scratched and our privileges taken away. Good Shepherd love is costly love. For additional help on these issues, read *Grace at the Table*,[3] available through Bread for the World, and my own book *Beyond Guilt*.[4]

Children's Time

Try exploring with the children the idea of being excluded, as a way of explaining what Jesus meant by "other sheep." Ask the children if they have ever been left out or excluded, and have them give examples. To help them start to think about it, give them a personal example from your life, or use puppets to tell a story about being left out. God doesn't want to leave anyone out. When people are hungry, they feel left out. Jesus wants us to help them so that they don't feel left out. What can we do?

Musical Suggestions [LH]

Brothers and Sisters of Mine Are the Hungry—BP 148

God the Spirit, Guide and Guardian—NCH 355

Now It Is Evening—FWS 2187

The City Is Alive, O God—PSH 597

Jesus, Shepherd of Our Souls—GC 725

3. David Beckmann and Arthur Simon, *Grace at the Table* (New York/Mahwah, N.J.: Paulist Press, 1999).

4. George S Johnson, *Beyond Guilt: Christian Response to Suffering* (Cambridge, Minn.: Adventure Publications, 2000).

George S Johnson

Fifth Sunday of Easter

RCL: Acts 8:26-40; Psalm 22:25-31; 1 John 4:7-21; John 15:1-8
LM: Acts 9:26-31; Psalm 22:26-27, 28, 30, 31-32; 1 John 3:18-24;
   John 15:1-8

Vines and branches were very familiar to first-century Palestinians. Many of them worked as peasants in vineyards. Their backs got tired from picking and hauling grapes to market. They knew the story in the Torah in which Israel is pictured as God's choice vine, and they were familiar with the expectations of the landlord (Isa 5:1-7). God looked for good grapes, not wild grapes. God looked for justice, not a cry from people who were exploited.

John's epistle reminds us that love of neighbor is the chief fruit expected from the vine. Any branch that does not produce is in danger of being cast aside. Sometimes pruning is needed so that the productive branches can yield even more. Pruning is not pain free or easy or always desired. Sometimes God calls us out of our comfort zone to reach out to neighbors, and in doing so our belief systems are called into question, our politics challenged, and our ways of doing things exposed as paternalistic or controlling. Even the way we read the Bible may seem economically biased. That's why advocacy work is hard and may not always be popular.

Jesus' audience knew all about pruning and growth. For John, the fruit of loving one's neighbor is a test, a goal, an expectation, and a reminder of one's calling.

The story of the vine and branches is a good foundation for lifting up the needs of hungry people, as well as for our responsibility to act in order to address those needs. Knowing God, loving neighbor, and doing justice are always linked in the Hebrew Scriptures (Jer 22:16; Isa 58:6-10).

The gospel and epistle readings help us to remember that believing and loving one's neighbor are part of the same truth. To believe is to love, and to love is to believe. They are not so much cause and effect as two ways of talking about the same experience. Then John steps out on a limb and makes a bold statement: "Everyone who loves is born of God and knows God" (1 John 4:7). Our tendency is to reverse it and say that whoever is born of God will love. For John, believing (being born of God) and loving one's neighbor cannot be separated or lined up as first and second. Loving our neighbor is a sign that God's Spirit dwells in our lives. Our actions will speak much louder than our words or creeds.

Jesus lived the true nature of love. He noticed who had been excluded and identified with the people society had cast aside. This was Jesus' option for the poor. Joerg Rieger points out that the part of humanity that does not have a share in the structures of privilege and power is also prevented access to the centers of theological reflection and to the benefits of society.[1] These are the ones Jesus noticed, talked about with his disciples, and loved by identifying with them. To help in our own noticing, membership in Bread for the World can keep us more aware of what is happening among those who are excluded today.

Society puts a high priority on reducing taxes and consuming to keep the economy going. We tend to look for ways to protect our investments and secure our safety before we look to our neighbor's needs. So this love of neighbor, this fruit God is looking for, is not always that easy or popular. It involves asking hard questions and being aware of the long-range consequences of our decisions and our lifestyles. Jesus' kind of love always carries with it an economic dimension.

Ched Myers says that the economic implications of the Gospel story comprise three axioms:

• The world that God created is abundant, with enough for everyone.

---

1. Joerg Rieger, *God and the Excluded: Visions and Blindspots in Contemporary Theology* (Minneapolis: Fortress Press, 2001).

- Disparities in wealth and power are not "natural" but the result of human sin, and must be mitigated within the community of faith through the regular practice of redistribution.

- The prophetic message calls people to practice such redistribution and is characterized as "good news" to the poor.[2]

José Miranda, a Mexican economist and theologian, examines the word "glory" in the Old and New Testaments.[3] He shows that glory *(doxa)* is linked to God's justice, to God's acts in history to liberate from oppression (Isa 58:8b; 62:2a; Ps 97:6). God is glorified when justice is done for poor and oppressed people. We remember Paul's words in Romans 3:23: We "all have sinned and fall short of the glory of God."

We love our neighbors together, not only individually. When we join others in efforts to combat hunger in activities like letter writing or a Hunger Walk, we express a community love of neighbor. The Church, not just individuals, is called to love, even as Israel was called to be a blessing to the whole world. A kind of solidarity builds when we joins hands with others who are seeking to alleviate world hunger. We may not agree on doctrine or the sacraments, but acting together in loving our neighbor can unite us as a body with Christ as the head. CROP Walks are a good example. Bread for the World unites Christians from a wide variety of creeds and traditions. Working together, we make a difference.

Children's Time

Pass out either candy or grapes or small pieces of something the children would like to have—give one person many and the others only one. Then ask, "What do you think I should do so that all of you will be happy? What do you think this person who has so much should do? If he or she were to take the many and give some to all the others so that each had about the same number, what would you call this?" Recognize the answers. (Help the person who has much do this.) Then

2. Ched Myers, *The Biblical Vision of Sabbath Economics,* a booklet published by The Church of the Saviour, Washington, D.C., under the heading "To Tell the Word" (2001) 5.

3. José Miranda, *Marx and the Bible: A Critique of the Philosophy of Oppression* (Maryknoll, N.Y.: Orbis Books, 1974).

suggest another term that we sometimes use—"redistribute." When someone has more than they need and some don't have any or not enough, God wants us to share or redistribute. When we give money or food to help poor and hungry people, we are redistributing our wealth. That is what God asks us to do as part of what it means to love our neighbor and to show God's love in our hearts. Suggest that the children ask their mom or dad if they can bring some food from their kitchen to redistribute so that those who have little will not go hungry. With God's help we can do that.

Musical Suggestions [LH]

I Am the Vine—GC 672

Source and Sovereign, Rock and Cloud—CH 12

We Are Called—GC 718

The Fallow Heart Is God's Own Field—BP 193

George S Johnson

Sixth Sunday of Easter

RCL: Acts 10:44-48; Psalm 98; 1 John 5:1-6; John 15:9-17

LM: Acts 10:25-26, 34-35, 44-48; Psalm 98:1, 2-3, 3-4; 1 John 4:7-10; John 15:9-17

Today's gospel follows directly from that of the Fifth Sunday of Easter and the image of the vine and branches. John writes about seventy years after Jesus' death and here recalls Jesus' final message to his disciples. Last words before parting are always important, often summarizing what has been said or taught. Jesus doesn't want his people to forget some very important lessons concerning their calling to love their neighbor. Our calling to care for poor and hungry people is rooted in Jesus' final words before going to the cross. Importante!

Some key concepts in this text include:

Abide in my love (15:9). "Abide" suggests a place to remain, a home base, a point of reference, a lasting source from which to draw energy, a center not to be abandoned. When we center on love, we are not as prone to make ethical decisions out of greed, revenge, or prejudice. Our home base, the place from which we see the world, makes a difference in our perception and course of action.

Remembering the radical nature of Jesus' love refocuses his disciples on the needs of poor people around them. They know that some will resist when they preach Good News for those who are poor. Abiding in Jesus' love means to persevere in countering the dominating and controlling powers that keep some people from experiencing abundant life.

It means not leaving home base, God's love. It means always testing one's motivation.

Keep my commandments (15:10). We may be reluctant to talk about commandments as important to Gospel preaching. Preachers of the Gospel don't want to become legalistic and moralistic or betray the doctrine of grace. But Jesus certainly talked about the demands of a healthy relationship, about obedience. He summarized all the commandments into two: love God and love your neighbor. To abide in his love is to keep these commandments. Walter Brueggemann reminds us that there is an element of demand in our relationship with God. He calls it "the delight of duty."[1] When God's love touches us, this command becomes our delight. We don't have a choice to love or not to love those who are poor and hungry in our society and our world. Obedience cannot be separated from grace in our relationship to God. Our obedience becomes Gospel to those in need.

My joy may be in you, and your joy complete (15:11). Loving one's neighbor may not always be easy or fun. It often involves hard work, it taxes our minds, and sometimes it's even painful. But the promise we claim from verse 11 is that doing the right thing toward our neighbor brings a satisfaction that can be called joy. In part, this comes from knowing that God is in charge, even when our efforts are rejected or ignored. This joy needs to be celebrated. Those working to end hunger need to gather from time to time just to celebrate, to sing, to dance, and to give room for that joy to be experienced.[2] Bread for the World's National Gatherings offer opportunities for such celebration.

No one has greater love than this, to lay down one's life for one's friends (15:13). Love is a word with many meanings today. In this verse we encounter the dimension of suffering—deeply—with the person in pain. A group leader once asked me if I could honestly say that I would lay down my life for the person sitting next to me. I swallowed hard. Should I be honest? I wanted to say yes because I remembered what Jesus said and what Christians are expected to do. After a pause I said no. Of course, I had my good reasons. All our love for our neighbors may come up short, but we know what and who our model is, what our goal is, the direction our love may take us. The Christ within us may

---

1. Walter Brueggemann, *The Covenanted Self* (Minneapolis: Fortress Press, 1999).

2. For good resources and ideas on celebration, see Elsa Tamez, *The Scandalous Message of James: Faith Without Works Is Dead* (New York: Crossroad Publishing, 2002) 170–71.

stretch us from time to time. Where is our need for stretching today in seeking to love those who are poor and hungry?

No longer servants, but friends (15:15) When love for neighbor matters, it has a different motive and orientation toward the "other." Our relationship to our neighbor, the Gentile, the excluded takes on new meaning. It doesn't fit the master-servant, top-down, paternalistic attitude that often characterizes our approach toward the Third World. We are not better or more loved or more blessed because we have more. The term "friend" is not meant to give us a cozy feeling of intimacy with Jesus, but to empower us to love our neighbor as Jesus did. We sing "What a friend we have in Jesus." Knowing that we meet Jesus in our needy neighbor, we can also sing "What a friend we have in our neighbor in need."

Children's Time

How many of you have friends? Tell me the name of one of your friends. About how many friends do you have? You may have someone who used to be your friend but is not your friend anymore. Friends are important, aren't they? What makes a person a friend? Jesus once said to his disciples, "You are my friends." That must have made them feel good. Then he added these words: "if you do what I command you." We all know what Jesus commanded—to love our neighbor, to love one another. Friendship is a relationship. Friends are people we love and who love us. Learning to love our neighbor is a way of making friends. It makes us feel closer to our friend Jesus. There are hungry children in our world looking for a friend who will love them enough to share their food with them and to stand up for them in their struggle to survive. Maybe you would like to take the picture in today's insert in the bulletin and hang it in your bedroom to remind you of someone who wants to be your friend. Draw me a picture of friendship and bring it with you next Sunday.

Musical Suggestions [LH]

Filled with the Spirit's Power—UMH 537

I Come with Joy—CH 420

Help Us Accept Each Other—PH 358

Un mandamiento nuevo—NCH 389

Called as Partners in Christ's Service—PH 343

George S Johnson

The Ascension of the Lord

RCL: Acts 1:1-11; Psalm 47 or Psalm 93; Ephesians 1:15-23;
Luke 24:44-53

LM: Acts 1:1-11; Psalm 47:2-3, 6-7, 8-9; Ephesians 1:17-23 or 4:1-13
or 4:1-7, 11-13; Mark 16:15-20

Ascension Day may be a time when the rational side of us wrestles with the assigned text. Knowing that some have given up on the institutional Church after hearing too many sermons on "heaven up there" and "men in white robes," we look for ways to preach about Ascension that speak to our everyday lives here and now. Can this text call for change in our way of seeing the world so that love of neighbor and God's justice are the intended outcomes? I think so. Pray for wisdom and courage as you prepare.

Luke sets the story in the context of Jesus' disappearance, his physical absence from the disciples. It takes place forty days after the resurrection, forty-three days after his death and burial. Where did the risen Christ go? Why didn't they see more of him if he did indeed come back alive? Who will lead them now? What is their next move? They experience Jesus' powerful presence in the post-resurrection appearances, but those seem sporadic and uncertain. The Ascension tells how the early Church understood the resurrection and learned to cope with the absence of Jesus' physical body.

A key concept in the Ascension text is the "kingdom of God," mentioned in verses 3 and 6.[1] The kingdom is the center of Jesus' message

---

1. See such sources as William Herzog II, *Jesus, Justice and the Reign of God* (Louisville: Westminster/John Knox Press, 2000), and Richard Horsley and Neil Asher Silberman, *The Message and the Kingdom* (Minneapolis: Fortress Press, 1997).

and mission, but at times the disciples have trouble understanding what it means—as do we. We pray for it to come every time we pray the Our Father: "Thy kingdom come." When we unpack the meaning of the kingdom of God, we are getting at the main issue of the hunger and poverty in our world. The kingdom is the reign of God, where justice is done, where people experience the abundant life, where no one needs to go hungry.

Justice is the right ordering of all our relationships—to self, to God, to neighbor, and to creation. At the heart of those relationships are equity, compassion, and freedom. Jesus knows that where poverty prevails, justice and the reign of God are absent. For this reason we see him again and again embodying an option for poor and excluded people.

Unfortunately, the concept of oppression is not a major theme in much of the theological training offered in the First World. There are more than three thousand references to it in the Bible, where it's identified as the main cause of hunger and poverty. What we see in the Scriptures depends on where we stand. From the position of privilege in the world, we often read the Bible with our own economic lenses, so oppression is not a major theme in our biblical exegesis. It should be. Our sisters and brothers in the Third World can help us read the Bible again.[2]

The Ascension text's main theme is the proclamation in Acts 1:8: "You will receive power." Power to love as Jesus loved. Power to love our neighbor who is hungry and naked and homeless. Power to do things we could not do on our own. Power to lay down our lives for others. Power to resist. Power to persevere. Power to engage the powers of domination and exploitation. Yes, the issue is power, but a different kind of power. There is a scene in the movie *Schindler's List* in which a German officer is about to kill an innocent youth to show his superior power. Schindler proposes to the officer that true power is the power not to inflict violence when one could. Gandhi said that nonviolence is the weapon of the strong. Acts 1:8 tells about those kinds of power.

This leads us to the Holy Spirit and lays the ground for Pentecost Sunday. This power to love is a radical fruit of the Spirit. It is the presence of Jesus in our lives, a presence the disciples experience after Jesus is no longer physically present. What Jesus had come to show them—another way—is now to be carried on through their witness to the ends

2. See chs. 1–2 of Thomas Hanks, *God So Loved the Third World: The Biblical Vocabulary of Oppression* (Maryknoll, N.Y.: Orbis Books, 1983), and Robert McAfee Brown, *Unexpected News: Reading the Bible with Third World Eyes* (Louisville: Westminster, 1984).

of the world. This other way involves sensitivity to people's hurts and needs, feeding hungry people, and addressing society's inequalities. Jesus offers this as a "Third Way," an approach that Walter Wink talks about in his book *Engaging the Powers*.[3] The book of Acts witnesses to how Jesus' disciples followed this Way as they distributed to all in need.

We witness by our talk and by our walk. I once took a group of young people to Tecate, Mexico, where they spent a week at an orphanage. Language was a barrier at first, but before long it was evident that there is a universal language, the powerful language of love. The youth from Texas and Washington were witnessing to God's love through their actions, their attitudes, their tears, their playfulness, and their smiles. Lives were changed, energized, and opened to new realities. It was a Pentecost experience again. God's grace flowed both ways. It was Acts 1:8 in action.

Children's Time

Bring a bicycle up front so the children can see it. Ask them if they know how to ride a bike. Ask who helped them learn how to ride one? Was it scary? They most likely had seen someone else ride a bike and said, "I can do that too." At first maybe their mom or dad held on to the bike, but then they let go, right?

Jesus came to show us how to love our neighbor. Then it came time for him to leave us. He said: "Now I want you to carry on for me and be my witness. I want you to love your neighbor just as I have loved you. Okay?" The time when Jesus let go of the bike and told us to carry on is called Ascension Day. Jesus was still there with the disciples, but in a different way. Today Jesus is still with us, even though we can't see him. And he wants us to carry on. That means we are to help poor and hungry people in Jesus' name. That is what Jesus would do and what we can do. "Don't be afraid," he says, "I will be by your side at all times."

Musical Suggestions [LH]

Canticle of the Turning—GC 556

You Are Mine—FWS 2218

As We Gather at Your Table—FWS 2268

World without End—GC 532

3. Walter Wink, *Engaging the Powers* (Minneapolis: Fortress Press, 1992).

George S Johnson

Seventh Sunday of Easter

RCL: Acts 1:15-17, 21-26; Psalm 1; 1 John 5:9-13; John 17:6-19

LM: Acts 1:15-17, 20a, 20c-26; Psalm 103:1-2, 11-12, 19-20; 1 John 4:11-16; John 17:11b-19

This Sunday's gospel takes us into Jesus' heart as he prays for the disciples. The depth of his feeling and concern is beautiful. He seems to anticipate the struggles his followers will face, knowing the forces that will resist the alternative way he has taught them. His prayer strengthens us in our struggle to live out our love for the neighbor.

The term "world" in the gospel (17:14) refers to the powers and systems of domination in society, which suggests why "the world has hated" the disciples and "they do not belong to the world." Yet the same word embraces God's inclusive love (John 3:16).

This might be a good Sunday to take a fresh approach to the texts by preaching on the psalm. Psalm 1 is a good place to reflect on the struggle to bring about changes to help alleviate hunger and poverty. The psalm introduces the choices we make that are related to the powers and systems Jesus talks about in his prayer in John 17. This psalm, which introduces all the psalms, pictures two ways, two kinds of people, two choices, two results. Jesus also talks in the Gospels about two paths, two gates, two masters, two foundations, two consequences, two interpretations, and two allegiances. We will make a difference in the world if we resist the powerful pressures that cause suffering and if we make wise decisions and choices. Some key phrases in the psalm shed light on these choices.

Happy are those. Not everyone today is happy, nor have we all found the meaning to our existence. Happiness comes to those who . . . who what? The wording seems to suggest we have a choice, and decisions to make. God's Word constantly invites us to choose the way of life. The psalm suggests that we continually face choices about whom to follow, what to follow, what path to take—choices that impact on who eats and who doesn't eat. People ask why this is so and how our choices make a difference. One choice we can all make is to care about poor people as much as the Bible does. Consider introducing your parish to the Generous Christian Pledge that Ron Sider promotes.[1]

The wicked, the righteous. It all seems so obvious and easy to choose. Who in the world would decide to be wicked? Maybe the hardened criminal or some perverted person, but not any of us who attend worship. The psalmist seems to make it all beautiful and ugly, the right and wrong way. Yet don't our choices often seem to land somewhere in between? We can't always clearly identify evil and good. Our consumption of material things and our indifference to, or ignorance of, the degradation of the environment aren't evil, are they? What are those sins we confess in our prayer of confession—"things we have left undone" and "We have not loved our neighbor as ourselves"? Can we show how our choices lead to life or to death of God's creation, God's children, our neighbors? The psalm can also be a call to repent of our bad choices.

Delight in the law of the Lord. When God's grace touches people, when they say yes to the invitation to follow Jesus, they speak about a delight, a desire, a thirst for doing the right things. It is a delight that rests in justice and peace. We can substitute "justice" for "the law of the Lord," because the Torah is the book of God's ordering of right relationships (justice). Delighting in the law of the Lord means being willing to see that justice is done for those who are hungry and poor. Here is a good place to discuss how letter writing to elected leaders on behalf of hungry people can be a delight in the law of the Lord.

They are like trees. Trees, water, fruit, seasons are all familiar things from nature, from God's beautiful creation. Each can become a teaching symbol, reminding us how choices we make affect our relationships. We often neglect our relationship to the environment, the earth. Both the godly person and the Church are called to be good stewards

---

1. Ron Sider, *Just Generosity* (Grand Rapids, Mich.: Baker Publishers, 1999) 221.

of creation.[2] When we are about good stewardship, trying to find out what our neighbor needs, we are like a tree receiving and giving, bearing fruit in season. A tree-planting ceremony some Sunday after worship can help celebrate the church's decision to be an eco-justice community that delights in the law of the Lord and serves as a lesson in patience.

The Lord watches over. This is about hope. Our choice to follow the way of justice brings a sense of God's presence and allows us to live out the image of God within us. In the struggle we do not lose heart because we know that the earth is the Lord's. That's enough.

Children's Time

After showing the children a picture of a tree, ask them: "Do you know how many trees are around your house? What is your favorite tree? Why? Have you ever climbed a tree? Have you ever seen a tree house? Are there fruit trees in your yard? Why do birds like trees?"

Today's psalm says that people who follow the way of God's commandments are like trees that have water, that bear fruit in season, that give shelter and shade, that breathe and help humans to breathe. What does it take for a tree to be healthy, to bear fruit? Talk about this for a moment.

People who are like trees are the ones who delight in doing what is right in God's eyes. They delight in learning about God's Word, in learning how to love God and neighbors. We can become like trees that bear fruit as we study God's Word and as we share with hungry and poor people. When someone asks you why you go to Sunday School, say it's because you want to be like a tree that bears fruit. Those trees need good water and the sunshine of God's love.

Musical Suggestions [LH]

O Christ Jesus, Sent from Heaven—NCH 47

Come and Find the Quiet Center—FWS 2128

The One Is Blest—PH 158

For the Fruit of All Creation—BP 91

---

2. For a broader meaning of the stewardship concept, see Douglas John Hall, *The Steward: A Biblical Symbol Come of Age* (New York: Friendship Press, 1985).

George S Johnson

Pentecost Sunday

RCL: Acts 2:1-21 or Ezekiel 37:1-14; Psalm 104:24-34, 35b; Romans
  8:22-27 or Acts 2:1-21; John 15:26-27; 16:4b-15

LM: Acts 2:1-11; Psalm 104:1, 24, 29-30, 31, 34; 1 Corinthians 12:3b-7,
  12-13 or Galatians 5:16-25; John 20:19-23 or 15:26-27; 16:12-15

Signs of death, pain, and hopelessness are all around us. In spite of
advances in science and technology, the world is still torn apart by
poverty, hatred, and violence. The Christian religion, not to mention
all the other religions, has had two thousand years to make a difference, to bring about change. But is the world better today? As one
looks out on the human landscape, it reminds us of the valley of dry
bones. And we ask, "Can these bones live?"

There is enough food in the world to feed everyone. Frances Moore
Lappé was correct back in the 1970s when she wrote her best-selling
book *Diet for a Small Planet.*[1] The myth of scarcity has been exposed
for what it is—a myth. Yet chronic hunger haunts over 800 million
people in our world. Why do 2.8 billion people live on less than two
dollars a day while the rich become richer? It is easy to despair, become
cynical, and give up hope. Yes, we can point to some progress through
efforts of organizations like Bread for the World, but the cry of hungry
people continues to ring in our ears.

If Pentecost means anything, it means don't give up hope. God has
not given up on us; God is active in this world bringing life out of death.

1. Frances Moore Lappé, *Diet for a Small Planet* (New York: Ballantine, 1975).

Jesus did not see the end of hunger and poverty in his lifetime and met a cruel death after only a few years of ministry. But Pentecost reminds us that God wants to bring life and hope to the dry bones of violence and despair.

The dry bones story comes alive by knowing the storyteller's setting, the context in Israel's history. The people are living in exile, away from home, and things look hopeless. Both Jerusalem and the Temple have been destroyed. For all the world it looks like God's promises have failed them. It is a valley of dry bones. In our day we can experience such despair reading the news or traveling to places of suffering in the Third World. Some 16,400 children die every day in the developing world from malnutrition and hunger-related causes, and there's no easy way to stop that tragedy. You may need to tell stories to make all this real to those of us who are privileged. So many things can keep us from listening to the cries of poor and hungry people. Ignorance must not allow us to live in denial.

But also tell positive stories. Frances Moore Lappé, in another book,[2] takes us into the Third World beneath the radar of the global media and shows how dry bones are coming to life in poor villages of Kenya, among landless peasants of Brazil, and for single mothers of Bangladesh. They are learning to survive by transforming fear into creative action. People have taken Ezekiel's story to heart. They have not given up hope, even though the market economy of globalization would say that it is a given that some should live in poverty.

"Mortal, can these bones live?" A testing, theological question. "Oh, Lord, you know." Is this a sufficient answer or an escape? When our friends or colleagues ask if we think there is any answer to the hunger problem, it is easy to despair—or answer in a way that puts the blame on God or on the victims. Some even use the Bible to justify passivity in the face of hunger's continued existence. People may give up hope unless we come with the confidence portrayed in this text. Continuing to write letters and work for a better life for the excluded ones means we believe that justice can live and be a reality.

Pentecost Sunday is about the hope-inducing presence of God in our real world. It is about the wind of God blowing new energy into our lives, into places where there appeared to be only death and decay. It is hard to describe, but you feel it and know it is real because it changes

2. Frances Moore Lappé, *Hope's Edge* (New York: Penguin Books, 2002).

lives. Go to the newspaper or to literature from your Church's hunger program and pick out a story of hope or amazement. Or tell the story of someone like Zacchaeus in Luke 19 or the Good Samaritan in Luke 10. Tell about the work of Bread for the World or Amnesty International or Habitat for Humanity or Call to Action or Ministry of Money. Be open to the transforming wind (Spirit) of God and to the bones coming together with breath and power.

Children's Time

One of today's Bible passages tells a story about dry bones. It tells how God can make dry bones have flesh and come to life. God can bring life where there is death. God can make a difference. God wants all of us to make a difference—and we can.

Today we're going to do something that makes a difference. I'll bet many of you haven't done this before. We're going to write a letter together. Okay? Here I have some paper and a pen. We're going to write to the President of the United States and ask him to help hungry people. We know that letters to our nation's leaders can make a difference by reminding them that people like you care about those who are poor and hungry. So what shall we write to the President? I'll write down what you suggest. Why don't we begin by thanking him for something. (Write down their ideas.) Now, what shall we ask him to do to help hungry people? (Wait for some ideas.) Good! Shall we remind him what we've learned in our Bible about helping people who are hungry. Good! Now each of you can print your name at the bottom, and we'll put this in the offering plate this morning as part of our offering to help hungry people. Thank you for helping us write this letter.

Musical Suggestions [LH]

Spirit—PH 319

Wind Who Makes All Winds That Blow—PH 131

Song over the Waters—GC 585

Let It Breathe on Me—NCH 288

Dem Bones, Dem Bones (Anthem)

Jim McDonald

Trinity Sunday

RCL: Today's Revised Common Lectionary readings are listed at the beginning of the reflection that pertains to them.

LM: Deuteronomy 4:32-34, 39-40; Psalm 33:4-5, 6, 9, 18-19, 20, 22; Romans 8:14-17; Matthew 28:16-20

Psalm 29: A meditation on God's power to communicate and on the power of God's communication. The Lord's voice is majestic. Are we listening? God can do amazing things! Do we believe it? The psalm is a kind of mini-liturgy, beginning with a bold call to worship and ending with a calm prayer of petition for strength and peace. But note the mayhem in the middle, when "the voice of the Lord" thunders. Look at the action verbs associated with that voice: it breaks, makes, shatters, flashes, shakes, strips, thunders! What power! Can we feel it? Do we hear God's voice over the din of the everyday? Have you noticed how the volume of TV commercials is louder than the programs they accompany? Hundreds of groups clamor for our loyalty and our action every day. They want us to buy, to join, to support financially and politically. They vie for our hearts and minds and time. But God's voice wants us to remember the centrality of God's glory.

And what is the glory of God? As Irenaeus said, "The glory of God is a human being fully alive!"[1]

Isaiah 6:1-8: The call of Isaiah. Verse 1, "In the year that King Uzziah died," invites us to consider the historical context in which God has called us, especially those events that unmoored us from our familiar view of the world. Isaiah's vision in the temple is fantastic and awe-inspiring; the splendor of God's holiness and glory fills the whole earth, the temple of the Lord. An Isaiah-like vision also prompts our call as peacemakers and justice-seekers. But the very splendor of the vision makes Isaiah and us feel unworthy: "Woe is me! I am lost, for I am a man of unclean lips, and I live among a people of unclean lips" (v. 5). The passage shows that God calls us for two reasons: because God needs us and wants to change us. To paraphrase Gandhi, we must expect that we will become the change we seek. We are not simply message-carriers; we are the message itself, a message in progress.

Romans 8:12-17: Paul tells how Jesus Christ has fundamentally changed our lives, since in him God has adopted us into the family as one of God's own. This is a totally new relationship, with a new set of expectations. All our relationships change, not just our relationship with God. We become a child among children, an heir among heirs. Our whole family looks different, and how we treat others must change to reflect that new reality. When we open ourselves to the Spirit—of life, of God, of Christ—and let the Spirit dwell in us, we are set free from the old rules, expectations, and behavior patterns that governed our lives. Our social actions should affirm those changes. If the hungry person is really our brother or sister, how do we bear witness to that fact? If those who are living on less than a dollar a day in Mozambique, Haiti, or Vietnam are really members of our family, how should our country's foreign policy reflect that reality?

John 3:1-17: God's Spirit moved Nicodemus out of his comfort zone. A devout member of the Jewish Sanhedrin, a leader in the religious establishment of that time, Nicodemus had a lot to lose by his association with Jesus. So he comes to Jesus by night. What attracts him is his sense that Jesus "has come from God." His instincts tell him that he can learn something important from this unordained "Rabbi," as he

1. Robert Ellsberg, *All Saints* (New York: Crossroad, 2000) 279; see Irenaeus, "An Exposition of the Faith," in Cyril C. Richardson, ed., *Early Christian Fathers* (New York: Macmillan, 1970).

calls him. Imagine, then, Nicodemus's reaction when Jesus tells him that being born once is not enough if one is to see the kingdom of God. To understand God's work in the world, one needs to be born a second time, in a different way: by the Spirit, "from above." God doesn't move according to the pronouncements of Church councils or by the declarations of religious leaders. God's Spirit works like the wind, blowing where it chooses. It's blowing even now in *our* world! Can we hear it? Are we open to its urgings, even if it moves us in uncomfortable ways? John 3:16 doesn't say, "For God so loved the Church . . ." It says, "For God so loved the *world*"! John 3:17 doesn't say that God condemns the world, but that God sent his Son into the world to save it. God doesn't call us to church membership; God calls us to become fully human by following Christ, serving and loving others. There's a big difference between church work and the work of the Church. The former keeps us busy maintaining an institution, while the latter takes us out of our comfort zones and sends us into the world to join the work of God's Spirit, making all things new. Eternal life is not what happens when life ends; it's what happens when life begins through the grace and mercy of Jesus Christ.

Children's Time

• Teach the children the Avery and Marsh song "I Am the Church, You Are the Church."

• Have them act out Psalm 29 using percussion instruments, clapping, movement, etc., to dramatize the action verbs and illustrate how God tries to get our attention. Ask them why they think God needs to try so hard to communicate with us.

• Ask them if they know anyone who has been adopted. Talk about what a wonderful thing adoption is.

Musical Suggestions

Breathe on Me, Breath of God—BP 88

Holy, Holy, Holy! Lord God Almighty!—PH 138

Spirit of the Living God—BP 103

Lord, You Give the Great Commission—BP 106

I, the Lord of Sea and Sky (Here I Am, Lord)—BP 129

Jim McDonald

Ninth Sunday in Ordinary Time

RCL: Today's Revised Common Lectionary readings are listed at the
   beginning of the reflection that pertains to them.
LM: Deuteronomy 5:12-15; Psalm 81:3-4, 5-6, 6-8, 10-11;
   2 Corinthians 4:6-11; Mark 2:23–3:6 or 2:23-28

Psalm 139:1-6, 13-18: The operative word in this part of the psalm is
"wonderful" (vv. 6 and 14, twice). God's deep knowledge of us leads
to our deep affirmation of ourselves, which is to say of all human beings that they are "fearfully and wonderfully made" (v. 14). There is
no escaping God's notice, whether we like it or not. Sometimes we are
assured by the knowledge of God's constant care, sometimes we are
annoyed, and sometimes we are frightened. God knows it all—past,
present, future; the good, the bad, the ugly. But the amazing, wonderful thing is that God never gives up on us, never stops loving us, or
trying to help us become the wonderful human beings that we were
created to be. God asks us to have the same attitude toward all who inhabit this world. The psalm is a call to confession, honesty, and truth-
telling; to integrity, healing, reconciliation, and wholeness. God's grace
makes it all possible and compels us to respond.

1 Samuel 3:1-10 (11-20): Samuel's call comes before dawn, during a
dark time of political crisis, when the nation's rulers have forgotten that
they are accountable to God. The religious establishment is in decay as
well, its leaders uninspired and feckless. Nonetheless, God's presence
and power stir in a young, spiritually alive boy named Samuel (Jewish

tradition says he was twelve). At first Samuel is confused, thinking it's the voice of Eli the priest. But Eli grasps the import of the moment and helps Samuel understand that it is God speaking. Ironically, the message God delivers to Samuel spells doom for the house of Eli. At first afraid, Samuel accepts the role of prophet, choosing to speak God's truth to God's people, regardless of their reaction or response. Just when no one thinks it possible, God raises up a new generation of religious leadership to revitalize the nation and change the course of history. These are often the dynamics at the dawn of a movement for social justice.

2 Corinthians 4:5-12: Paul's eloquent defense of himself and his ministry captures an essential reality for those engaged in ministry: "We have this treasure in earthen vessels to show that the transcendent power belongs to God and not to us" (v. 7, RSV). We who try to follow Christ and serve God are human beings—inadequate, inconsistent, flawed, limited. Every group, every institution is likewise imperfect. We forget, make mistakes, and fall down on the job. We overestimate our capabilities and underestimate the entrenched interests behind the status quo. Nonetheless, we have a treasure to offer: "the light of the knowledge of the glory of God in the face of Christ" (v. 6). The good news of the Gospel—God's reconciling, redeeming love—motivates us. The treasure remains resplendent, even in the earthen vessel. Our efforts to minister in Christ's name, to work for changes in public policy that will improve the lives of poor and hungry people, may seem feeble and inadequate in the face of the overwhelming needs and powerful, well-heeled interests that seem to control the political process. We may find ourselves under attack—"too liberal, too conservative, too naïve, too political, too whatever." Still we press on, "bloodied, but unbowed," because we have faith that the life Jesus offers will shine through our ministry.

Mark 2:23–3:6: The Sabbath was made for humankind, not humankind for the Sabbath. But the religious leaders of Jesus' time have it backward. They think that the purpose of faith in God is to make human beings pious followers of rules, "goody-goodies." So when Jesus takes grain from the fields to feed his disciples and heals a man with a withered hand on the Sabbath, the religious authorities attack him. Jesus reminds them that feeding hungry people and healing the sick are holy acts. Meeting human needs is an act of worship. Sabbath, of course, is the day of rest, a day set apart to remind us that life is fundamentally an unearned gift of God. Genesis 1 says, "On the seventh day God finished his work." The ancient rabbis concluded, however, that there was an act of creation on the seventh day as well—happiness, serenity, tranquility, harmony, peace (*menuha* in Hebrew, usually translated as "rest"). Sometimes when church members try to involve their congregation in Bread for the World's Offering of Letters, they meet resistance from pastors or members who believe the Church should "steer clear of politics." But hunger isn't a partisan issue. And when people write letters urging our nation's decision makers to take action to help parents feed and educate their children or poor countries fight poverty, hunger, and disease, they join themselves with God's purposes. What better way to observe the Sabbath?

Children's Time

- Discuss how important it is to be a good listener—to each other, our parents, grandparents, God. Like Samuel, sometimes we need someone else to help us understand something we've heard that doesn't quite make sense.

- Show them the book *The Faces of Jesus* with the commentary by Frederick Buechner (Croton on Hudson, N.Y.: Riverwood Publishers; New York: Simon and Schuster, 1974). Discuss several African, Asian, or Latin American depictions of Jesus. Tell them that all around the world there are people who love Jesus because they have discovered how much Jesus loves them. Tell them that Jesus doesn't care whether we are rich or poor, old or young, black, brown, red, yellow, or white; he loves us all just as we are.

- Talk about the importance of a day for God (Sabbath). Tell them how important it is to take time to appreciate and celebrate God's creation and to thank God for being alive and being loved. Tell them to ask their parents to take them for a walk in the woods or to sit with them on the porch some summer evening and just look at the stars.

Musical Suggestions

Lift Ev'ry Voice and Sing—BP 177
Be Thou My Vision—BP 99
God of Grace and God of Glory—BP 175
Precious Lord, Take My Hand—PH 404

Jim McDonald

Tenth Sunday in Ordinary Time

RCL: Today's Revised Common Lectionary readings are listed at the beginning of the reflection that pertains to them.
LM: Genesis 3:9-15; Psalm 130:1-2, 3-4, 5-6, 7-8; 2 Corinthians 4:13–5:1; Mark 3:20-35

The readings for this week are about matters of the heart—the unseen way in which God is reshaping our lives and our world. They challenge our twenty-first-century American propensity to want immediate, tangible, demonstrable results for our efforts. We believe that if we can't see it happening, it's not happening. But as the German sociologist Max Weber once reminded us, "Politics is a strong and slow boring of hard boards."[1] So, too, with social justice. God doesn't call us to be effective; God calls us to be faithful. The rest is in God's hands.

Psalm 138: The psalmist gives profound thanks as he assesses how God has made a difference in his life. "I give you thanks . . . with my whole heart" (v. 1). Contrast that with our halfhearted gratitude! Look at all the reasons he gives. This God on high associates with the lowly, actually seems to *prefer* such an association to the entitlement, exclusivity, and privileges such an exalted status allows. This God is attentive, hearing his cry and answering, though he walks in the midst of trouble. Who might the enemies of the psalmist be? The character of this God, who is above all others, is good news for those who are the

---

1. Max Weber, "Politics as a Vocation," in *From Max Weber: Essays in Sociology,* trans. and ed. H. H. Gerth and C. Wright Mills (New York: Oxford University Press, 1946) 77–128.

least, the lowly, the marginalized, the poor. This God's character strengthens their souls. Who might this psalmist be today?

1 Samuel 8:4-11 (12-15) 16-20; (11:14-15): The crisis of political and religious leadership continues. Samuel has become like Eli; he is old and his sons are scoundrels. Israel wants a king to govern them, like other nations. Dismayed, Samuel prays. Dismayed, God answers. The discussion between Samuel, God, and the people of Israel sets out our timeless ambivalence about government. In a perfect world we would need no government because everyone would serve the God of creation and redemption, doing justice and loving-kindness. But the people of Israel know that they do not live in a perfect world. They want a government to establish the rule of law, protect its citizens, and provide for the common welfare. Samuel argues that governments do not automatically serve the people and instead can become corrupt and oppressive. Yet God and Samuel decide that the people should have their way. It becomes incumbent upon the people of Israel to establish the government they want and to make it work for them, in accordance with God's purposes. This challenge is still ours today: to make governments serve God's purposes and all God's people, especially those with the least.

2 Corinthians 4:13–5:1: Of his ministry, Paul tells the Corinthians, ". . . we do not lose heart" (4:16). Why? Because God's process of salvation is hidden, not obvious. If you look for the conventional signs of progress, if you measure success by the world's standards, then your ministry—your work for justice, your peacemaking, your public advocacy for poor and hungry people—will appear to be a failure. But we know better because changes that matter—changes of the heart—come slowly, almost imperceptibly. On a daily basis, it can seem to us that the world is going to hell in a handbasket or that we have run into a brick wall. Life and ministry can be difficult. Working for justice can be discouraging. But the problems we encounter, the suffering we endure, the setbacks we experience should be seen as "slight momentary afflictions." The work of ministry is not a steady progression toward a measurable goal by a certain time. It is participating in the hidden process of God's salvation so that "grace, as it extends to more and more people, may increase thanksgiving" (4:15). Take heart!

Mark 3:20-35: The unforgivable sin is to blaspheme the Holy Spirit. Why? The first three chapters of Mark's Gospel make it clear: Jesus, filled with the Holy Spirit, is doing battle with the unholy, unclean spirits of our world. The unclean spirits have captured and twisted the human spirit. Jesus has come as the healer of body and soul, to drive out the unclean spirits and make room for the life-giving Holy Spirit. Jesus' ministry is a ministry of liberation, of freeing the captives from the demons that possess them. The work of the Holy Spirit—the ministry of Jesus—is creating a whole new human family. Unfortunately, this new creation threatens and confuses the old order, still possessed by unclean spirits. Jesus, however, is undeterred. He affirmed then, and affirms today, that those who do God's will are members of God's whole new human family. That means us, as we carry on Jesus' liberating work.

Children's Time

- Begin by reminding the children of the saying, "Sticks and stones can break my bones, but words can never hurt me." But then acknowledge that words, in fact, do hurt sometimes—not physically like sticks and stones, but they can wound our spirits. Talk about words that hurt. Acknowledge that sometimes when we are angry or hurt, we use words to try to hurt other people. Remind them that we ought to measure our words.

- On a piece of newsprint, draw a symbol of a heart ♥. Talk about different images of heart: broken, rapidly beating, heartburn, big, stopped, and finally what "losing heart" means. Tell them how important it is never to lose heart.

Musical Suggestions

God of Justice, God of Mercy—BP 86

The Lord Hears the Cry of the Poor—BP 109

When the Poor Ones (Cuando el Pobre)—BP 154

Every Time I Feel the Spirit—BP 212

Jim McDonald

﹡

Eleventh Sunday in Ordinary Time

﹡

RCL: Today's Revised Common Lectionary readings are listed at the beginning of the reflection that pertains to them.

LM: Ezekiel 17:22-24; Psalm 92:2-3, 13-14, 15-16; 2 Corinthians 5:6-10; Mark 4:26-34

Psalm 20: This psalm is a prayer offered before a person or group embarks on an important mission. A couple leaving behind family and friends to work with poor people? A church council considering how to respond to its neighborhood's needs? A Bread for the World covenant congregation undertaking an Offering of Letters campaign? Before beginning work each day or before considering the next steps in a struggle for justice, before leaving for a new peacemaking endeavor or before undertaking a huge campaign to change the politics of hunger, we should gather to pray for one another and for our common purpose. At the core of our petition is this: "May [God] grant you your heart's desire" (v. 4). Our heart's desire is not a momentary wish or a fleeting emotion; it's not a brief institutional advantage or the ephemeral ascendancy of a political party; rather, our heart's desire is an abiding, burning passion to see God's reign on earth.

1 Samuel 15:34–16:13: David's anointing. This is a good text to use when considering leadership. Leaders sometimes go against type. Some who we suppose would make great leaders turn out to be too egotistical, self-absorbed, or controlling. Others who almost escape our notice because they are unassuming, unpretentious, or unlikely become the right persons at the right time. What makes a great leader and what criteria should we use when we search for leaders? "The LORD looks on the heart" (16:7). Israel has endured Saul's disastrous and unstable reign, and even God rued choosing Saul! (15:35). But God works through Samuel to find Saul's successor, sending him to the house of Jesse in Bethlehem, one of Judah's little clans. Among Jesse's sons, God chooses the youngest, one unproven in battle, a shepherd boy. The rest, as they say, is history—salvation history.

2 Corinthians 5:6-10 (11-13) 14-17: Paul is living according to a new reality. Christ's love explains everything and motivates all we do: "The love of Christ urges us on." "We walk by faith." "We are always confident" (vv. 6, 7, 14). It's also the lens through which we view everything. Everything looks different—the world, our lives, other people, even Christ! Why? Because we have come to understand that Christ's death and resurrection draw a bright line between the past and the future. Christ's death wipes out the old, and his rising brings a whole new creation that truly offers new life to everyone. Paul invites us to live with him in this new reality too.

Mark 4:26-34: How do we understand the reign of God? Ever since calling his disciples, Jesus tries to show them what it means to live a life of faith in God. He heals those who are sick, invites outcasts to dinner, teaches people how to forgive, shows people how to share their resources of food, money, and compassion. He's trying to show how faith can mend what is broken and redeem what is lost, breaking down barriers between people and opening doors to new possibilities. Faith calls people to risk themselves for the sake of others, creating new lives and new communities.

Now Jesus sits down with his disciples to help them process what he has done and what they have seen. He doesn't lecture them or prepare a Bible study or ask them to attend synagogue; rather, he speaks in parables, using the language of everyday life to open them to the hidden way in which God is working in and through him, them, and the world. We hear two parables: the seed growing secretly, manifesting itself in different forms at different times; and the mustard seed, the smallest of seeds, which grows big enough to become a sanctuary for the birds of the air. What might these parables say to those of us who become impatient or discouraged as we work to overcome racism, homophobia, or indifference to hunger and poverty? For example, think about the state of racism in the United States in 1830, 1863, 1896, 1935, 1954, 1965, and today. Is there a seed that has been growing? Is the seed still growing today?

When I was young, it seemed I was always aspiring to be like someone older. When I was six, I wanted to be seven. When I was a sophomore in high school, I wanted to be like the seniors. As a high school senior, I thought college kids were the cool ones. In college I believed that it was the people out in the "real" world who were really making a difference. As a seminarian, I couldn't wait until I was ordained so that I could be a "Minister." Freshly ordained, I wanted the experience of those in community or presbytery leadership positions. Now I realize that the best age is the one you are. God's Spirit has been working through me at every age and every stage. I only wish now that I had been more aware of that then.

Children's Time

- Tell the story of "little David," the boy David—harp player, shepherd, obedient son, giant slayer.

- Ask, "Why do we pray?" Discuss different times for prayer and various kinds of prayer. Tell them that we pray, not to get what we want, but what we need. Sometimes when we don't know what we need, when we're confused, prayer helps us to discover what we need.

- Bring a jar of mustard seeds and give one to each child. Talk about what happens when you plant a mustard seed in the ground. Ask them about little things they can do for someone else that might mean a lot to that person.

Musical Suggestions

Lord, How Can We Feed a Hungry World? (Mustard Seed Faith)—
  BP 156

Sing a New Song Unto the Lord—BP 137

Cantad al Señor (O Sing to the Lord)—PH 472

God, You Spin the Whirling Planets—PH 285

Jim McDonald

Twelfth Sunday in Ordinary Time

RCL: Today's Revised Common Lectionary readings are listed at the beginning of the reflection that pertains to them. This week includes alternative Hebrew Scripture and psalm readings: 1 Samuel 17:57–18:5, 10-16; Psalm 133.

LM: Job 38:1, 8-11; Psalm 107:23-24, 25-26, 28-29, 30-31; 2 Corinthians 5:14-17; Mark 4:35-41

Psalm 9:9-20: The psalmist appeals to the God of power and justice for liberation from oppression and evil. Throughout its history the tiny nation of Israel had an unshakable belief that God neither forgets nor forsakes the poor, needy, and afflicted ones. Verse 9 affirms that God is a "stronghold for the oppressed." A stronghold is a place of security, a sanctuary where one can go to be safe and to survive. But God is not simply a lifeless rock behind which to hide. God is an advocate who takes up the cause of the oppressed (vv. 9-10, 13, 18). In North American churches, however, sanctuaries are too often viewed as places of safety and security rather than places of transformation and liberation. What God do we come to worship when we gather as a community of faith?

1 Samuel 17:(1a, 4-11, 19-23) 32-49: David and Goliath. The little guy slays the giant! Those who work for social justice and a better world often feel they are fighting just such battles with the odds stacked against them. The enemies are huge—money, power, and the indifference to suffering they can breed. Our resources are meager—the faithful action

131

of the committed few. So what is David's secret? First, David has confidence in his own experience and abilities. Second, he recognizes that he owes his past successes to the power of the living God working through him. So David discards the armor and weapons that Saul tries to bequeath him in favor of what he knows will work for him—five smooth stones and his slingshot (vv. 38-40). David confronts Goliath, not to achieve glory for himself or even his tribe, but on behalf of the whole people of God and as a witness to the God of justice.

2 Corinthians 6:1-13: Paul caps his appeal to the Corinthians with a plea for understanding, reciprocity, and, ultimately, solidarity. "Our heart is wide open to you," he tells them (v. 11). Paul challenges the Corinthians to respond faithfully to his ministry with their own concomitant ministry. "Open wide your hearts also" (v. 12). To make this passage come instantly alive, imagine it is an appeal from a group of poor or oppressed Christians to another group of rich Christians living in a powerful nation. Imagine, for example, Archbishop Desmond Tutu writing this to the Church in North America. What would he be asking from us? Across the centuries, in many parts of the world, Christians have put their lives on the line to witness to the Gospel. From their suffering they appeal to others, even us, to examine our own fidelity to the Gospel. Solidarity asks that we remove the artificial barriers ("no restriction in our affections") that separate us from one another—barriers of nation, race, class, and gender—and join our hearts and hands in prayerful, hopeful, concerted action for justice and peace. In their 1997 reflection *Called to Global Solidarity,* the U.S. Conference of Catholic Bishops noted that "our parishes often act as islands of local religious activity rather than as parts of the mystical body of Christ." They remind the faithful that "solidarity is action on behalf of the one human family, calling us to help overcome the divisions in our world."[1]

Mark 4:35-41: Fear and faith. The boat journeys in Mark take Jesus and the disciples back and forth across the Sea of Galilee between two sections of Israel that are very different from each other politically, socially, and religiously. In his ministry Jesus tries to bridge the gap between these two disparate groups, but as Ched Myers and others note

1. The entire reflection is available at http://www.nccbuscc.org/sdwp/international/globalsolidarity.htm.

in their commentary on this story, "Mark's harrowing sea stories suggest that the task of social reconciliation was not only difficult but virtually inconceivable."[2]

As the storm hits their boat, the panicked disciples wonder aloud if the sleeping Jesus cares. When Jesus awakes, he talks not to the disciples but to the wind and the sea, that is, to the (spirit of the) storm itself. Then he chastises the disciples for their fear and lack of faith. He cares all right—enough to calm the storm (their fears) so that they can complete their journey. But ultimately he cares more about the strength of their faith. How difficult it is sometimes for us who profess our faith in Christ to undertake and complete the difficult work of reconciliation.

Children's Time

- Talk about the logo of the Children's Defense Fund with its prayer: "Dear Lord, be good to me. The sea is so wide and my boat is so small." (www.childrensdefense.org)

- Retell the story of David and Goliath in your own creative way.

- Talk to them about praying when you are afraid. Remind them that God is with us even when we are afraid.

- If your church has a (sister) relationship with a church in another part of the world, this would be a good Sunday to talk about that relationship and why it's important.

Musical Suggestions

In Christ There Is No East or West—BP 87

The Lord Hears the Cry of the Poor—BP 109

Bless, O Lord, Your Country, Africa (Prayer for Africa)—BP 147

You Shall Cross the Barren Desert (Be Not Afraid)—BP 208

---

2. Ched Myers and others, *Say to This Mountain: Mark's Story of Discipleship* (Maryknoll, N.Y.: Orbis Books, 1996) 57.

Jim McDonald

Thirteenth Sunday in Ordinary Time

RCL: Today's Revised Common Lectionary readings are listed at the
beginning of the reflection that pertains to them.

LM: Wisdom 1:13-15; 2:23-24; Psalm 30:2, 4, 5-6, 11, 12-13;
2 Corinthians 8:7, 9, 13-15; Mark 5:21-43 or 5:21-24, 35b-43

Psalm 130: A penitential psalm with powerful affirmations, this is a
call to Hope, with a capital "H." It is not enough to hope for small
things, for changes that seem possible. The hope we place before God
comes from an aching sense that the world and we ourselves are far less
than we could or should be. We hope for a world without hunger, war,
or oppression. "Out of the depths I cry to thee" (v. 1, RSV). No suffering is too great to separate us from God. "If thou, O Lord, shouldst
mark iniquities, Lord, who could stand?" (v. 3, RSV). No one—not
anyone—merits God's favor. "But there is forgiveness with thee, that
thou mayest be feared" (v. 4, RSV). No sin or evil deed is too heinous
for God to forgive. And thus, "My soul waits, and . . . I hope" (v. 5).
Emily Dickinson wrote: "Hope is the thing with feathers / That
perches in the soul, / And sings the tune without the words, / And
never stops at all."[1] We hope "more than those who watch for the
morning" (v. 6). We hope for redemption, for a New Creation, as we
pray and wait. And so we live and work for justice and peace.

2 Samuel 1:1, 17-27: David grieves the deaths of Saul and Jonathan.
The father and son were killed in battle with the Philistines (1 Sam

---

1. Emily Dickinson, *The Complete Poems,* Part I: Life, Poem 32 (Boston: Little, Brown,
1924).

31:2-4). Though Saul was a controversial figure in Israel's history, David honors him unabashedly with a song of lament. David also honors his close relationship with Jonathan, as well as lamenting Jonathan as a person. The content of these verses seems less important than David's act of mourning. Our culture attempts to minimize the need to grieve our losses. But grieving is necessary work because it purifies our hearts and creates the space wherein the Spirit of hope can come and dwell. Grieving brings to mind the things that made someone unique. Grieving helps rid us of distortions about the past and gives our lives a more honest perspective. We can prize the ways we have grown, the things we have learned, the goodness we have touched, the gifts we have been given, and the love we have shared. Grieving helps us in our moment of loss to name and define our experience in the past so that we can grab the best of it and bring it with us into the future, leaving the rest behind. David's grieving sets the stage for his reign as Israel's greatest king. Our grieving may prepare us for new works of advocacy as a way to honor those we have lost and join ourselves with the purposes of God. Many social movements and organizations around the world have just such a genesis. Can you think of some?

2 Corinthians 8:7-15: Paul educates the church in Corinth on the meaning of stewardship. The previous year that church, apparently relatively well-off financially, had started to raise money, along with several other congregations, to help the Jerusalem church. The churches in Macedonia, though quite poor, had contributed to the effort, even beyond their means. But for some reason the Corinthians hadn't completed their part of the effort. Now Paul is trying to goad them into finishing, without commanding it (v. 8). At stake here is not just the task of "raising the money"; rather, it's the motivation behind the money. Paul wants to infuse their giving with the spirit of generosity (see vv. 2 and 7). He equates grace and generosity; both are the uninhibited, unconditional outpouring of ourselves for others in love, as Christ did. Paul wants there to be a fair balance between abundance and need. If we take Paul's words about "abundance and need" to heart in today's world, what would that mean about the amount of money we give away personally, as a church, and as a nation? Whose wealth is it anyway?

Mark 5:21-43: A powerful story of healing, personal and social. Two daughters are healed—one, the twelve-year-old daughter of a prominent religious leader; the other, an older woman of limited means, probably at the margins of Galilean society, who had become destitute unsuccessfully seeking medical care over the past twelve years. These two women and the way in which they came to Jesus' attention couldn't have been more different. What is striking is that Jesus does not allow Jairus's privilege, prominence, and pleading to dim his sensitivity to the poor woman's plight. Poignantly, Jesus calls her "daughter," reminding her—and us—that she is part of the community. Then, just as he had to challenge the social stigmas of class and gender to heal the older woman, Jesus challenges the social ignorance that denies the possibility of healing for Jairus's daughter. Both rich and poor need healing, and both can be healed in Jesus' name.

Children's Time

Read a children's book on death and grief, such as Judith Viorst's *The Tenth Good Thing About Barney,* illustrated by Erik Blegvad (New York: Aladdin Books, 1987), or Charlotte Zolotow's *My Grandson Lew* (New York: Harper & Row, 1974).

Musical Suggestions

Hope of the World—BP 176

There Is a Balm In Gilead—BP 132

Canto de Esperanza (Song of Hope)—PH 432

By the Waters of Babylon (or By the Babylonian Rivers)— PH 245 or 246

God, Whose Giving Knows No Ending—PH 422

Jim McDonald

◼

Fourteenth Sunday in Ordinary Time

◼

RCL: Today's Revised Common Lectionary readings are listed at the beginning of the reflection that pertains to them.

LM: Ezekiel 2:2-5; Psalm 123:1-2, 2, 3-4; 2 Corinthians 12:7-10; Mark 6:1-6

Psalm 48: The God of time and place transcends time and place. The God whose beauty can be seen in God's city, the holy mountain, will be Israel's God and guide forever. When the congregation ponders God's steadfast love (v. 9), they feel secure, able to survive any challenge, accomplish any task.

2 Samuel 5:1-5, 9-10: David becomes king over Israel and Judah "because the Lord . . . was with him" (v. 10). Here we glimpse the interplay between God's grace and purposeful human striving, even ambition. God's blessing of David from the very beginning of his life gives David a deep confidence in himself, a strong inner drive to succeed and become a leader. But David does not become great overnight. He has a lot to learn, which only experience can teach. Gradually, he grows ever more impressive as a person and a leader, eventually earning his mandate to rule. Thus when the elders of Israel come to David,

137

entreating him to fulfill his calling, David is ready and responds immediately. Great political leaders, including David, know that they are accountable both to God and to the people they govern. David makes a covenant with the elders of Israel before they anoint him king. Political leaders are dependent on God's grace. They must also exercise power care-fully, knowing that they have been entrusted with the sacred responsibility to establish and uphold the well-being of the entire community they serve. Our advocacy should be a reminder to our nation's leaders of this sacred trust they hold.

2 Corinthians 12:2-10: Paul's thorn in the flesh. William Sloane Coffin once remarked that in life "there are things hoped for and things we are stuck with."[1] Thorns in the flesh are painful reminders of our mortality and human frailty, showing that life is not something we can control and that forces greater than ourselves are at work in the world—to keep us "from being too elated" (v. 7). Some thorns are physical, but most are invisible to the naked eye. How do we come to terms with "the things we are stuck with"? Paul says he went to the Lord three times about his thorn. That suggests patience and perseverance, but my guess is that Paul did not approach God with a quiet spirit. In the end God tells Paul, "My grace is sufficient . . . for my power is made perfect in weakness" (v. 9). This is not an easy message to absorb. What are the things we consider weak? How do we respond to weakness in ourselves? How can Paul be such a powerful, important figure in the early Church if he is so weak? Is weakness really necessary for God's power to be made perfect?

Mark 6:1-13: The cost of discipleship. The Church is often tempted to preach exclusively the attraction/attractiveness of Jesus. This story of Jesus' rejection by his own kith and kin in his hometown is an antidote reminding us that Jesus' ministry can threaten the status quo. Jesus comes to establish a new kind of human family and a new sense of human community. To do that he needs disciples—those willing to receive his teaching and healing power, and use it to teach, heal, and cast out demons in his name.

But the cost of discipleship is high. The road is treacherous; the journey, tortuous. We can become discouraged by the enormity of the task, disheartened by our apparent lack of resources. We can allow our

1. William Sloane Coffin, *The Courage to Love* (San Francisco: Harper & Row, 1982) 24.

failures to convince us that success will never come. For just such reasons, Jesus offers his disciples a set of rules for the road. First, travel light. Trust that God will give us what we need as we go, and avoid the temptation to possess, consume, or hold on to the past. Second, travel together. As we respond to God's call, inviting others to come with us accomplishes the same things it does for police officers who work in teams: it provides accountability, safety, and companionship. And it makes for a more powerful witness. Third, travel in peace. A healthy sense of calling is not that we are charged to end racism or violence, or eliminate hunger, or find a cure for AIDS, or solve the problems of family life, but rather that each of us has a contribution to make in some important way toward those goals.

Children's Time

Discuss the word "disciple." What does it mean to be a follower? Have they ever played "Follow the Leader"? What was it like? How can we follow Jesus?

Musical Suggestions

I Sing the Almighty Power of God—BP 230

Do, Lord, Remember Me—BP 121

'Tis the Gift to Be Simple—BP 167

Amazing Grace! How Sweet the Sound—BP 105

Let Us Talents and Tongues Employ—BP 213

Elizabeth Vander Haagen

Fifteenth Sunday in Ordinary Time

RCL: 2 Samuel 6:1-5, 12b-19; Psalm 24; Ephesians 1:3-14; Mark 6:14-29

LM: Amos 7:12-15; Psalm 85:9-10, 11-12, 13-14; Ephesians 1:3-14 or
   1:3-10; Mark 6:7-13

The theme of holiness can be traced throughout today's passages. Gail Godwin, in a fascinating book of essays called *Heart,*[1] describes the Hebrew concept of holiness as "whole-heartedness." This is an excellent definition of the justice God desires and will one day bring about, when people will be whole-hearted in their love for God, others, themselves, and the world.

In the reading from 2 Samuel, David and the people honor God's holiness, transporting the ark of God to the political capital, Jerusalem. They celebrate the whole way with music and sacrifices. At the height of their worship, David distributes food among all the people of Israel, men and women. Throughout Scripture, food is a sign of God's favor and a symbol of covenant. It is significant that David gives the people a blessing along with their food and that all the people receive enough. God recognizes the significance of food and desires that all be fed. This passage illustrates the biblical combination of worship, celebration, and action/service. The prophets remind us that God is not interested in worship separated from action, and this celebration illustrates the point.

1. Gail Godwin, *Heart: A Natural History of the Heart-Filled Life* (San Francisco: Harper Perennial, 2002).

140

Psalm 24 includes the themes of holiness and worship. The psalmist affirms that God is the source and sustainer of life and all that nourishes it. When the psalmist asks who is worthy and holy enough to stand before this God, the answer is telling: those with clean hands and pure hearts. Again, the link between worship and action is clear—those who live rightly may approach God.

The Sweet Honey in the Rock song "Are My Hands Clean?"[2] invokes this psalm, suggesting that none of our hands are clean because we all contribute to injustice. This shouldn't keep us from the work of advocacy, but instead should inspire us to live as justly as we can. The song describes a garment's journey from the cotton fields of Central America to the fiber mills of the southern U.S., where the cotton is combined with thread made from South American oil. Later the garment is assembled in a Haitian sweatshop and sold at a discount in a U.S. department store. We're moved to ask, "Who gets rich and who remains poor from our purchases? What do our purchases cost us? What do they cost those who make them, particularly in terms of well-being?"

The epistle reading continues the themes of holiness, worship, and blessing. We are richly blessed in Jesus Christ, having been adopted into God's family and redeemed. Redemption is full of economic connotations: to redeem something is to pay for it, usually to pay off a debt. In Christ we have an example of lavish giving. In grateful response, we are inspired to give lavishly of our time and resources to others in the struggle against hunger and injustice.

The tragic story of John the Baptist's death also contains the theme of holiness. John's holiness, his whole-heartedness toward God and others, fascinates Herod. But this can't protect John from Herod's lust and his need to make a good impression. Often those who speak prophetically and identify wrongdoing by those in power (as John does by pointing out the questionable relationship between Herod and Herodias) take a great risk and do so at great cost.

Today's first reading from Amos in the Catholic Lectionary also illustrates this. Amos's prophetic words, calling the people to account for their mistreatment of poor people, do not fall on open ears, and the priests try to get rid of him, suggesting he eat his bread elsewhere.

---

2. Composed for Winterfest, Institute for Policy Studies. The lyrics are based on an article by Institute fellow John Cavanagh, "The Journey of the Blouse: A Global Assembly." Lyrics and music by Bernice Johnson Reagon, Songtalk Publishing Co., 1985.

Yet Amos remains faithful to the task God gives him, speaking truth to government, religious, and social leaders, reminding them that God demands justice of individuals and nations. This passage also reminds us that God calls people from all walks of life (including dressers of sycamore trees) to be spokespersons for justice on behalf of those who are hungry.

Psalm 85 poetically expresses the eschatological vision of the kingdom of God—justice, peace, and wholeness in the world. These promises, which include abundance from the fields and plenty to eat, provide hope in the struggle to end hunger and injustice.

Today's reading from Mark stresses that the call to discipleship sometimes means radical simplicity. Here the twelve disciples are sent on their journey without extra food or clothes. Sometimes following Jesus requires a different, simpler lifestyle, which is particularly difficult to do while living in North America. It is interesting that Jesus clearly communicates to the disciples that they are not responsible for how people respond to them. If they are not received, those who are inhospitable will have to answer for it someday. We may find this comforting when our pleas for justice seem to fall on deaf ears.

Children's Time

Most children are familiar with the daily routine of hand-washing, and the importance of clean hands for eating, etc. A children's sermon might include questions about what the psalmist means by clean hands and what cleanness has to do with praying.

Musical Suggestions [LH]

What Gift Can We Bring—UMH 87

Let Justice Flow like Streams—NCH 588

Lead Us from Death to Life—NCH 581

'Tis the Gift to Be Simple (Simple Gifts)—BP 167

Elizabeth Vander Haagen

Sixteenth Sunday in Ordinary Time

RCL: 2 Samuel 7:1-14a; Psalm 89:20-37; Ephesians 2:11-22;
Mark 6:30-34, 53-56

LM: Jeremiah 23:1-6; Psalm 23:1-3, 3-4, 5, 6; Ephesians 2:13-18;
Mark 6:30-34

 Today's passage from 2 Samuel reminds us of God's delight in reversals. God chooses one of the lowliest people in the land—the youngest son, a shepherd—to be king. When this king, David, wants to build a house for God, God again turns things around and says, "I'm going to build you a house—a dynasty—instead." Among the basic desires many of us share is to have children and to leave something behind for them when we die. This is what God promises David.

In our day, one of the realities in the cycle of poverty is the lack of inheritance for the children of poor people; there aren't enough financial resources to save and pass on. Micro-enterprises in many developing nations are changing this. Nonprofit organizations offer small, low-interest loans that provide the capital necessary to begin a small business. The small business owners (often women) become financially independent, pay back the loans, and in a few years can come to a point where they can save for the future. Action and advocacy can help provide funding and support for micro-enterprises in Third World countries.

In the passage from 2 Samuel, the prophet reminds David of God's identity as rescuer from the oppression of Egypt and of his own humble roots. We, too, are called to remind those in power that God is the God of the Exodus, the one who rescues from oppression.

Psalm 89 celebrates the same things: God's steadfast promises for David and for God's people. It includes images of this world—the seas, the rivers, and the heavens—as places where God is active. Knowing that God is active in our world is a source of hope in our struggle to end hunger and injustice.

The epistle reading also calls to mind God's previous reconciling acts. Speaking to Gentiles welcomed to the church, Paul says, "Remember the story of how you were once strangers to God's people, the ones God rescued from slavery in Egypt, and how God rescued you, also, in Jesus Christ. Remember that you didn't earn what you have. Your identity, your hope, your possessions are all from Christ." Out of remembering comes generosity: if we didn't earn what we have but have received it as a gift, we can freely share the gift with others. Christ reconciles those who have been divided by walls of class and culture. Do we live as though we've been reconciled? What might reconciliation look like in terms of the way we use our resources—do we share only with those who are like us or also with those who are different? The passage also speaks about God's house. If we are being built into God's dwelling, our life together should reflect God's hospitality and generosity. Finally, the passage speaks of citizenship. We are citizens of God's household more than of a particular nation. Bread for the World provides tools for us to be stewards of our citizenship, using our ability to influence our nation's leaders in ways that reflect our heavenly citizenship.

The gospel points us to the One who offers compassion to his tired and hungry disciples and to the crowds that seek him. His compassion leads him to cross both cultural and class boundaries and to go to Gennesaret, a Gentile area, to heal those who are sick.

The Catholic Lectionary's reading from Jeremiah deals with Israel's leaders. The biblical concept of righteousness and justice has to do with right relationships—with God, with neighbors, with self, and with the created world. God here rejects leaders who practice wickedness and do not pursue right relationships. The leaders have allowed injustice and hunger to flourish, letting the people wander away from God. God cares passionately about the decisions that national leaders make. The passage ends with God's promise of a time when a just and righteous one—the one we find in Jesus Christ—will appear and restore all relationships completely. Fear, violence, and injustice will be no more. The people will live with security.

Knowing that God cares deeply about the decisions our leaders make calls us to action on a national level. Knowing that God has promised a day when things will finally be as they should be gives us hope in the struggle to end hunger and injustice.

Children's Time

A children's sermon could include remembering together some of the stories of God: Noah, the Exodus, etc. Ask the question, Why is it so important to remember stories?

Psalm 23, the Catholic psalm for this day, is the most familiar biblical passage. Note the images of God's physical care and of food in the psalm. God is preparing a table for us! God not only uses food as a symbol but God is concerned with our most basic needs. Tim Ladwig has illustrated this psalm in a beautiful book.[1] He puts Psalm 23 in an urban setting, showing that God's protection, care, and concern are everywhere, including places of poverty and need. This book would be excellent to read as a children's sermon.

Musical Suggestions [LH]

Community of Christ—NCH 314

O Praise the Gracious Power—PH 471

We Are God's Work of Art (Somos la Creación de Dios)—GC 808

Come Away with Me—FWS 2202

The Fallow Heart Is God's Own Field—BP 193

---

1. Tim Ladwig, *Psalm 23* (Grand Rapids: Wm. B. Eerdmans, 1997).

Elizabeth Vander Haagen

■

Seventeenth Sunday in Ordinary Time

■

RCL: 2 Samuel 11:1-15; Psalm 14; Ephesians 3:14-21; John 6:1-21

LM: 2 Kings 4:42-44; Psalm 145:10-11, 15-16, 17-18; Ephesians 4:1-6; John 6:1-15

In today's Old Testament reading from 2 Samuel, the unpredictable and unacceptable happens. David, to whom God has provided blessings and wonderful promises, who has seen God at work and who is known as a person after God's own heart, uses his power to take advantage of another man's wife and then to arrange that man's murder. Injustice breeds a cycle of violence. David unjustly uses his power to take and have sex with Bathsheba. To cover up his actions, he calls Uriah back from battle and urges him to go to his wife. When Uriah refuses, David uses his power for violence again and has him murdered. The cycle of violence later continues to David's children. Injustice cannot remain hidden or be covered up by more violence. It always comes to light.

In today's psalm the singer recognizes that to mistreat people who are poor or those with less power is to act as though there is no God. Our actions show what we truly believe about God. God is identified in the psalm as one who sees when injustice is committed, who is with those who are poor, and who is coming to make things right! God is a refuge for people who are poor and for those who struggle against injustice and hunger.

The epistle reading brings back the theme of the importance of prayer and action together. Action and service spring from a deep relationship with Jesus Christ. The Christ who dwells in our hearts, according to Ephesians, is the same God who keeps company with poor and vulnerable people. What does it mean to be rooted and grounded in love? What does that look like in service and advocacy, and in our personal spirituality? The promises in verses 20-21 keep us going in our work to end hunger and injustice. God is able to end hunger and do far more than we can imagine!

The gospel reading from John is the story of the feeding of the five thousand. It is the only miracle story to appear in all four Gospels; everyone had heard about it, and it was so important that none of the authors wanted to leave it out. Feeding people is a sign of God's presence in the world and a key part of Jesus' witness and our witness to God's presence in our world. Jesus is profoundly concerned about people's hunger and basic needs. Though the disciples are overwhelmed and think it is impossible, Jesus makes a way for all to be fed and uses the efforts of the disciples (finding the resources of a few loaves and fishes) to do it. Distributing food is not based on the virtue of the receivers at all, but on their need and humanity. When all have shared, not only is there enough food, there is more than enough. Note that the story of the disciples in the dangerous storm comes right after the story of the miraculous feeding. Opportunities and needs don't go away, and we need Jesus' calming and generous presence with us to face them.

The Catholic reading from 2 Kings tells an Old Testament version of the same sort of experience. Elisha is faced with a crowd of a thousand needing food, and again, from seemingly meager supplies, God provides enough food for them. Scripture is full of stories about God feeding people—providing plants for the man and woman to eat in the Garden, giving Joseph the wisdom to store up food before the famine, sending manna in the wilderness for the people of Israel, and today's readings from 2 Kings and John. God clearly cares about people having enough to eat! We often ask and wonder if ending hunger is possible—we have a miracle-working God who longs to have all people fed.

In Psalm 145 we again see God's passionate concern and involvement with this world. God is the source of timely and abundant food and provision for all living things. God's people must share in the work of making sure everyone has enough. The last verses remind us again that throughout Scripture God hears the cry of those who are oppressed and responds by bringing liberation.

For comments on the reading from Ephesians 4, please see below, p. 150, under the Eighteenth Sunday in Ordinary Time.

Children's Time

Service and advocacy arise from a deep relationship with Jesus. A children's sermon could include telling the story of feeding the multitudes, with the visual aids of bread and fish.

Musical Suggestions [LH]

Pues Si Vivimos (When We Are Living)—PH 400

Let Us Talents and Tongues Employ—NCH 347

Time Now to Gather—FWS 2265

In the Singing—FWS 2255

Bread for the World—GC 827

I Saw the People Gathered—BP 151

Elizabeth Vander Haagen

Eighteenth Sunday in Ordinary Time

RCL: 2 Samuel 11:26–12:13a; Psalm 51:1-12; Ephesians 4:1-16; John 6:24-35

LM: Exodus 16:2-4, 12-15; Psalm 78:3-4, 23-24, 25, 54; Ephesians 4:17, 20-24; John 6:24-35

The passage from 2 Samuel tells us that God takes injustice very personally. Sinning against someone who is vulnerable is sinning against the Lord. Nothing done in secret is really hidden, and the Lord sends Nathan to confront David. David is upset with Nathan's story, but it isn't enough to be upset about injustice in the abstract or the injustice of someone else. Our own integrity matters. Again, God reminds David of their history together, of God's liberating acts, and of the proper response—gratitude, trust, and service. In Nathan we see the way God calls prophets and truth-tellers to use their skill to communicate God's message of justice.

Psalm 51 is David's prayerful response to the confrontation with Nathan. To transgress is to cross or violate a boundary. David violates the boundaries of marriage and takes what is not his to take. How do we as a nation or as individuals violate boundaries or take what is not ours? This psalm is primarily a prayer of confession. When we spend

149

time in confession, do we include participation in injustice as something for which we ask forgiveness as churches and individuals? Like David, when we recognize our participation in hunger and injustice, confession is the first response. Then the joy of salvation can return to us, and we can participate anew in God's liberating and reconciling acts through our advocacy and service.

Ephesians 4 describes the key characteristics of a Christian activist: humility (which can be especially difficult when you are more informed than others and feel passionate about something), gentleness, and patience (to persevere when you don't see results). The passage also talks about Christian unity, having one faith and one Lord. What does it mean to be one with the church in Zimbabwe, where people suffer famine and a huge percentage of the population is dying of AIDS? Or to be one with the church in Nicaragua, crying out for relief from the nation's unpayable debt? Doesn't it mean that we share deeply, intimately, in one another's struggles? Our unity expresses itself in a passionate concern for our hungry and oppressed brothers and sisters all over the world. If one part of the body is hurting, we all hurt, because we are one. The body metaphor speaks loudly when we think of hunger; parts of the Body of Christ are literally starving. What does it mean to be "one body" with them? The verses about gifts and equipping the saints remind us of our role in equipping fellow believers to be active and effective in the fight against hunger and injustice.

The context in which we hear or read Scripture often dramatically affects the way we hear or read it. How might the passage from John's Gospel for today sound in the ears of someone who is hungry? This passage points to the connections between food/sustenance, life, and Christ. The Jews expected that when the Messiah returned, he would renew the gift of manna, and Jesus has done that, but in a different way. Christ identifies himself as bread, that which nourishes and sustains life. As his followers, we participate in his work of nourishing and sustaining life in both a spiritual and tangible way.

The Old Testament reading in the Catholic Lectionary is the Exodus story of God's providing manna for hungry people in the wilderness. God hears when people cry for lack of bread. Throughout Scripture God is in the business of feeding people (see pp. 146–148), and food is a sign of God's care and provision for people.

In Psalm 78 the Israelites continue to hear of and tell their children the story of God's liberating work and nurturing care for them in rescuing them from Egypt and providing bread from heaven when they were in the wilderness.

The second reading in the Catholic Lectionary, from the letter to the Ephesians, describes the new self we are to put on. This new self is one that reflects Jesus, who calls us to feed hungry people, clothe those who are naked, and visit those in prison. The new self is in the likeness of God's righteousness, as the Holy Spirit guides us toward right relationships with God, others, ourselves, and the created world, relationships that are characterized by truth and justice.

Children's Time

A children's sermon could include examples of times we have taken things that are not ours. What can we do to make things right once we have taken them (say we are sorry, return what we've taken, etc.)?

Musical Suggestions [LH]

One Bread, One Body—UMH 620

When Minds and Bodies Meet as One—NCH 399

Let Us Be Bread—GC 816

Somos pueblo que camina (We Are People on a Journey)—NCH 340

Hope of the World—PH 360

Elizabeth Vander Haagen

Nineteenth Sunday in Ordinary Time

RCL: 2 Samuel 18:5-9, 15, 31-33; Psalm 130; Ephesians 4:25–5:2;
John 6:35, 41-51

LM: 1 Kings 19:4-8; Psalm 34:2-3, 4-5, 6-7, 8-9; Ephesians 4:30–5:2;
John 6:41-51

The lesson from 2 Samuel takes place during a civil war in Israel. David's son Absalom has gathered soldiers to take the kingdom from his father. Civil war often causes hunger in our world, and God and God's people are familiar with such conflicts. As is often the case, a cycle of violence and injustice is behind this civil war. Amnon, David's son and Absalom's half brother, raped Tamar, Absalom's sister. When David does nothing to punish Amnon, Absalom is outraged and murders Amnon and attempts to take David's throne. The civil war ends when Absalom is murdered in battle. David's grief reflects God's breaking heart and the stricken hearts of all victims of war's violence.

The psalm begins with a cry for help. God always hears the cry of oppressed people. Sometimes, as with Abel, God hears the blood crying out. With Israel in Egypt, God hears the nation's cry. Salvation his-

152

tory shows that God always hears the cry of those who suffer from injustice and is roused to action on their behalf. Here the psalmist sings of those who wait for morning.

One Easter I took part in a vigil in Love Park in downtown Philadelphia. The vigil was organized to protest the city's new anti-homeless laws, which made it illegal to sit or sleep in the park. We gathered at about 10 p.m. with blankets, hats, sleeping bags, coffee, and sandwiches to sleep out with the homeless people that night. All night policemen circled the park, and we waited for the morning, huddled in our sleeping bags, talking quietly with each other, wondering if daylight or arrest would come first. I've never waited and wanted morning to come so urgently. The psalmist describes such urgent waiting on the Lord, who has great power to redeem. God's power is capable of making right any wrong situation and is on our side as we advocate for justice and an end to hunger.

The epistle lesson underscores that people of faith have a unique calling to be truth-tellers. Part of putting away falsehood includes ending our denial about what our wealth and prosperity cost others. Studies I heard reported on National Public Radio show a direct connection between pollution in the Northern Hemisphere's industrialized nations and drought in sub-Saharan Africa. Putting away falsehood involves recognizing our corporate responsibility. The passage also speaks of anger, which is an appropriate response to injustice. The challenge is to channel anger into long-suffering love, as Christ did. Note also what this passage says about the purpose of work—to have enough to give to others. How would it revolutionize our communities if this became the purpose of our work? The passage ends with a powerful verse recited weekly by the deacon before the offering in Episcopal churches. What does it mean to give ourselves as a sacrifice to God? It means to spend ourselves—our time, energy, resources, and influence—on behalf of those who are poor and hungry.

The gospel lesson continues Jesus' claim to be the bread of life. Jesus provides more than literal, material bread, yet we know he also is deeply concerned with providing people with real bread. The passage connects Jesus with the Exodus event and the Eucharist. Manna in the wilderness and bread at the Lord's Supper are holy signs that in a mysterious way reveal God's grace to us. Jesus, as one who reveals God's grace, clearly makes unusual claims to satisfy both physical and spiritual hunger.

The Roman Catholic reading from 1 Kings is another feeding story, a sign of God's grace and blessing. Elijah, after defeating the prophets of Baal in the showdown on Mount Carmel, is running for his life into the wilderness. God sends an angel with food that sustains him on his long journey.

The first few verses of Psalm 34 bring to mind the Song of Mary (Luke 1:46-55), as God turns the world upside down. We can imagine Elijah singing a psalm like this as he eats in the wilderness. Food is an analogy for God's goodness: "Taste and see that the Lord is good" (Ps 34:8). Some Communion liturgies include this phrase, reminding us that in the Eucharist God's grace is present to us in a meal. If food is so important as a sign of God's goodness, making sure that hungry people are fed is central to the Church's witness for justice.

Children's Time

A children's sermon could include sharing some bread and remembering some of the stories in which God gives people bread (manna in the wilderness, feeding the five thousand).

Musical Suggestions [LH]

The Lord Hears the Cry of the Poor—BP 109

All Who Hunger—FWS 2126

I Am the Bread of Life—BP 124

Eat This Bread—UMH 628

Elizabeth Vander Haagen

Twentieth Sunday in Ordinary Time

RCL: 1 Kings 2:10-12; 3:3-14; Psalm 111; Ephesians 5:15-20;
John 6:51-58

LM: Proverbs 9:1-6; Psalm 34:2-3, 4-5, 6-7; Ephesians 5:15-20;
John 6:51-58

God is honored when we seek to do right, and God blesses those who keep covenant with him. In 1 Kings, Solomon praises David for his "righteousness," a word also translated as "justice." God expects and demands justice from those in power, and we are called to speak this truth to our nation's decision makers. Solomon is blessed, not for seeking wealth, but for seeking what is right. What would it look like if the desire to do right not only appeared in our political rhetoric but actually determined our nation's political priorities?

The psalm also connects justice and wisdom, praising God for being just and faithful and for saving the people from slavery in Egypt, making them into a new nation. The fear of the Lord—remembering God and God's power and desiring to do right—is the beginning of wisdom. Not only do the people remember God's works and covenant, but more importantly, God remembers the covenant, which includes

155

the expectation that the people care for poor and needy people and provide ways to ensure that all are fed.

The epistle continues the theme of wisdom, urging hearers to make the most of time. Reverend Eugene Callendar, the first African American minister in the Christian Reformed Church, quoted this passage in a sermon I heard him preach. He listed various systemic sins—racism and sexism among them—and after each one he called out to the people, "What time is it?" The people responded, "No time for foolishness!" The Spirit at work in this passage is the same Spirit Jesus spoke of in Luke 4, the Spirit that brings liberation to poor and vulnerable people. When we are full of the Spirit, an attitude of joy and gratitude permeates our work and our struggle for justice. No time for foolishness also means no time for cynicism and no time to waste!

The gospel lesson continues Jesus' claim to be the bread of life. Jesus makes explicit here the connection between life and food and himself as the source of eternal life. He also makes clear the connection between the Lord's Supper/Eucharist and life. What does it mean to celebrate the feast of the Lord's Supper in a world in which so many are hungry? To proclaim Jesus the source of life when people are dying of hunger? Feeding the hungry ones in our midst may be integral to being able to celebrate the feast.

The Catholic reading from Proverbs is also about a feast. Feasts in the Bible often mark significant events in the people's relationship with God. Whenever God makes a covenant with the people, they celebrate with a feast. Feasts marked the yearly festivals prescribed in the Law, particularly the Passover, celebrating the people's deliverance from Egypt and their birth as a new nation. Jesus gives his disciples a feast to remember him and likens the kingdom of God to a banquet to which all those who hear are invited. Here in Proverbs Lady Wisdom gives a similar invitation and likens wisdom to food—both are necessary for life. Often the problems of hunger and injustice are very complex and laws necessary to help are very complicated, yet wisdom is available to those who recognize their need for it.

Children's Time

A children's sermon could include talking about meals, and particularly special meals we share with others. Then you can explain Holy Communion as a special meal that reminds us of God's love.

Musical Suggestions [LH]

God the Sculptor of the Mountains—FWS 2060

Lord of Feasting and of Hunger—BP 141

How Good It Is—GC 727

Jesus, the Joy of Loving Hearts—NCH 329

Elizabeth Vander Haagen

Twenty-First Sunday in Ordinary Time

RCL: 1 Kings 8:(1, 6, 10-11) 22-30, 41-43; Psalm 84; Ephesians 6:10-20; John 6:56-69

LM: Joshua 24:1-2a, 15-17, 18b; Psalm 34:2-3, 16-17, 18-19, 20-21; Ephesians 5:21-32 or 5:2a, 25-32; John 6:60-69

The Old Testament lesson from 1 Kings includes Solomon's prayer dedicating the Temple. The God to whom Solomon prays is the one who has heard the people's cries, rescued them from slavery, and given them a covenant and laws to live as a just nation. The Temple is set aside as a sanctuary, that is, space that is holy and safe. In the Old Testament, places of sanctuary are safe for those running for their lives (see Numbers 35 and Joshua 20). Some churches in our day, particularly in states along our borders, have chosen to offer their space as sanctuary for undocumented immigrants. Solomon prays for the Temple's hospitality, that foreigners can come there and receive answers to their prayers. After September 11, 2001, there was a huge rise in anti-immigrant sentiment and propaganda in our nation. What might it mean for the Church to pray that immigrants would come and find answers to their prayers among us?

The kingly language in Psalm 84 reminds us that worship is always political. It always has to do with power, recognizing that power ultimately resides with God. The psalmist sings of God's care for small creatures as well as for people. I've seen this psalm illustrated in the Anglican Cathedral in Calcutta, India—a building full of contradictions. Walls are covered in memorials to British soldiers who died conquering and controlling India, yet on the same walls there are prayers for racial reconciliation and healing. The day I was there a young Indian girl was having a piano lesson on the cathedral's piano, while some sparrows were making a nest in the corner of one of the windows, where the stained glass was missing. As I left the cathedral, I noticed a small memorial to a priest who took part in the struggle for independence, whose prayers and those of others who were oppressed in India, were heard and answered.

The epistle lesson is about the armor of God and the struggle between good and evil. Dr. Martin Luther King Jr. spoke about the importance of nonviolent resistance—making truth known in a loving and firm way, recognizing that the enemy we struggle against is not people, but rather evil and injustice. Because this epistle was written from prison, it reminds us of the call to pray for and stand with those who are prisoners of conscience.

In the gospel lesson the disciples tell Jesus his words are difficult. Jesus' words and claims are, in fact, difficult; they demand a radical commitment to Christ and the ways of justice and mercy. Once again, Christ's affirmation as the true life is itself a life-giving word that inspires us in the struggle.

In the Roman Catholic reading from Joshua, God's saving the people from oppression in Egypt becomes the foundation of the relationship between God and Israel. The people repeat the story over and over again—this God liberated us and provided for us in the desert. The liberating, providing God who shaped the character and identity of Israel is the same God revealed in Jesus Christ. The same character and identity should be true of God's Church. As we live in solidarity with those who are suffering, we speak and act against hunger and injustice.

Psalm 34 is full of beautiful promises, reminding us that God's eyes and ears are open to those in need. Although this psalm includes promises of God's protection, it is interesting that it also assumes that those who obey the Lord will suffer afflictions. Those who advocate for justice will face hardship, yet they are promised that the Lord is near in the struggle.

The second reading in the Catholic Lectionary from Ephesians is about the most intimate of relationships, that of marriage. If we do not model love and justice in our closest relationships, we will not be able to practice it elsewhere. South Africa and the United States, which have histories of institutional racism, also have disturbingly high rates of violence against women, including sexual assaults. The way we relate to one another as men and women cannot be separated from our struggle against hunger and injustice.

Children's Time

A children's sermon can begin by asking the children what a jail or prison is and who stays there. Then explain why Paul was in prison, and talk about prisoners of conscience, like Dr. Martin Luther King Jr. Sample letters from Amnesty International supporting the rights of political prisoners could be made available to families after the service.

Musical Suggestions [LH]

You Satisfy the Hungry Heart—UMH 629

Lord of All Nations, Grant Me Grace—BP 178

I Myself Am the Bread of Life—GC 824

Bread of Life, Hope of the World—GC 821

Sister Christine Vladimiroff, O.S.B.

░

Twenty-Second Sunday in Ordinary Time

░

RCL: Song of Solomon 2:8-13; Psalm 45:1-2, 6-9; James 1:17-27;
Mark 7:1-8, 14-15, 21-23

LM: Deuteronomy 4:1-2, 6-8; Psalm 15:2-3, 3-4, 4-5; James 1:17-18,
21b-22, 27; Mark 7:1-8, 14-15, 21-23

How easy it is for religion to slip into myth, magic, and ritual, thus taming God's power to call us to greater fidelity and holiness. As religious people, we often engage in practices that distance us from God rather than draw us closer to God. When Jesus confronts the religious experts trying to entrap him, his central point is that the tradition of the elders is not the center nor heart of a relationship with God. The tradition itself is not the problem, but making it absolute and imposing its observance on others is. By divorcing tradition from the real intent, the Pharisees moved away from the deeper reality that gave the tradition life and meaning. They placed more value on what the religious institution created than the Word of God acting in their lives. They created idols out of practices that obscured God's work.

With very strong words from the prophet Isaiah, Jesus uncovers the scribes' and Pharisees' deception and invites us to assess our lives. Hypocrites are those who perversely and willfully mask their true attitude and intentions, performing what is acceptable in a given situation. They show a complete lack of integrity between what is visible to the public and what exists in their hearts. It is a life that is a lie. While the Pharisees and scribes are comfortable talking about laws and traditions concerning ritual purity and defilement, Jesus moves quickly into what matters—moral purity. True religion and character depend on authenticity.

The religion Jesus speaks of in today's gospel is a matter of the heart. It is about my openness to hear Jesus' challenge to live differently, to gradually succeed in bringing more harmony between the Gospel's demands and my life and actions. It is about my openness to the call of discipleship. It is a matter of relationship, built on trust and love.

This religion has the power to change a person and to transform our world.

We need to dwell on Jesus' words: "It is from within, from the human heart, that evil intentions come" (7:21). Good people lament the world we live in, a violent world that engages in war and a world in which children go hungry, immigrants are turned away from safe refuge, and the elderly are lonely. The task of discipleship is to transform this world into a place where God reigns. But as I look into my own heart, I recognize fear, coldness, alienation, anger, and the roots of violence. I seek a spiritual journey that will open me to God's converting love in my life and enable me to move to new levels of faith and forgiveness in my life with others.

That spiritual journey is best taken with others—in a community of believers. In community we find the mutual support to hear God's word in Scripture and change our hearts and our world. When God's word forms a community, it will connect with the world's pain, hardship, suffering, and injustice. The religious person is always a bearer of hope and refuses to let evil triumph.

In the days of the Cold War, buildings in our nation were designated as bomb shelters, with supplies of crackers for food, and we taught our school children, in the event of a nuclear attack, to hide under their desks for protection. Schools had regular drills to practice this maneuver. As a consequence, many children believed that they would never grow to be adults. Some even asked, "Mommy, where will you be when the bomb is dropped? Will you find me?" This fatalism among young people disturbed many psychologists. But they also found children who had not lost hope. When asked what they thought of the future and the possibility of a nuclear bomb hitting the United States, these children responded, "Oh, it is not going to happen because my mommy and daddy are working with other grown-ups to stop war and nuclear weapons." Significant adults in these children's lives were a source of hope for them. Through their words, but even more importantly by putting their love into action, these adults changed a threatening world into a safe world for their children. Religious people who have internalized Jesus' message do these transforming acts.

True religion enables us to fashion a world of love and caring, a society in which social justice, love, and compassion are so prevalent that violence becomes only a distant memory. By our actions we give witness to the heart-changing power of true religion. Fidelity to my relationship with God makes me responsible for doing justice.

Children's Time [LH]

Talk to the children about fear. Ask what they fear the most. They might answer that they fear the dark, or being lost, or not knowing where their moms and dads are, or big dogs that chase them. Tell them that it's natural to have some fears, that you had fears at their age and you still have some. But some things we don't need to fear because people protect us and because God cares for us, especially when we're afraid. That's because people like our parents and God love us and want us to be safe. When we're afraid we should tell God and our parents; they can help us feel better.

Musical Suggestions [LH]

O Young and Fearless Prophet—UMH 444

As a Fire Is Meant for Burning—GC 663

Come to Us—GC 743

Shepherd of Our Hearts—GC 829

Sister Christine Vladimiroff, O.S.B.

Twenty-Third Sunday in Ordinary Time

RCL: Proverbs 22:1-2, 8-9, 22-23; Psalm 125; James 2:1-10 (11-13)
14-17; Mark 7:24-37

LM: Isaiah 35:4-7a; Psalm 146:7, 8-9, 9-10; James 2:1-5; Mark 7:31-37

I have great admiration for the Syrophenician woman. First, she
has great love for her daughter, love that moves her to do the extraordinary. The woman does not let her Greek origin or her Gentile status
keep her from approaching Jesus and pleading for her daughter. Love
impels her to do the unthinkable.

Second, I admire her for the enormous hope and faith she has in
Jesus' power to heal. She stands before him in pure hope and falls to
her knees at Jesus' feet. Her very posture evidences the supplication
and trust she holds that Jesus can heal her daughter. She will not be
put off with Jesus' reluctance to heal a Gentile or be put down by Jesus'
words. With a quick wit she turns Jesus' phrase to her advantage. Her
hope is not disappointed, as her trust in Jesus' goodness and power
and her insistence gain her daughter's cure.

In today's second story, the crowd's faith brings healing to the deaf
and mute man. A community's faith leads it to seek Jesus so that he
can touch and open a person to hear and speak. God hears the plea because it comes with faith in God's power to act through Jesus. The
crowd stands in front of Jesus with pure hope that this can be accom-
plished, and they are not disappointed.

Where do I place my hope? With what confidence do I live my life
so that it conveys to others that God alone is my refuge and my hope?

How willing am I to do the audacious to bring goodness and healing to another? Can a community's faith bring goodness into the world of violence?

Thomas Merton wrote: "We are not perfectly free until we live in pure hope. For when our hope is pure, it no longer trusts exclusively in human and visible means, nor rests in any visible end. He who hopes in God trusts God, whom he never sees, to bring him to the possession of things that are beyond imagination."[1]

Our times test our courage and our capacity to hope. What we do with our pain, our frustration, and our hurt reveals the depth of our spirituality. We can move into a helpless, cynical mode, or we can go with faith to God. When we are at the edge, at a life juncture, that is where God's grace is and where transformation can take place.

In both miracles the prayer is for God's healing power to touch another person. The woman's love for her daughter brings her to Jesus, breaking all social taboos. The crowd brings the deaf and mute man to Jesus and with one voice asks Jesus to lay his hands on the man.

As committed disciples of Jesus, we need to be that healing touch in our world. I'm reminded of a story about a father who one night was babysitting his young daughter Millie. He put the child to bed and then sat down to read the newspaper. Suddenly a storm broke out, with thunder and lightning. From upstairs Millie called out, "Daddy, I'm scared! Come up and help me." The father, engrossed in the newspaper, called up, "Millie, you're safe. Remember, God loves you." Soon came another crash of lightning and thunder, and again Millie called from upstairs. "Daddy, I'm afraid and I know God loves me, but right now I want someone with skin on."

We can laugh at Millie's simple way of wanting to experience God through the loving presence of someone to protect her. But it's precisely when we express our compassion in action, whether sharing our bread with poor people, as we heard in Proverbs today, or working for justice in our economic and political structures, that we hasten the day when poor people will enjoy the earth's resources. These actions are living, convincing proof to others that we take our discipleship seriously.

How might I join my voice in a prayer of faith and hope that the burdens of oppression be lifted from those who suffer? How can I read today's Scripture and intercede in hope for a world of compassion and

1. Thomas Merton, *No Man Is an Island* (New York: Harcourt, Brace, 1955) 14.

justice? Am I willing to break social convention to intervene for another? Can I stand before God in pure hope and trust in God's goodness to hear me?

Children's Time [LH]

Talk about how hope is important in the Christian faith. Describe a way that hope changed the way you looked at a situation in your life and made a difference in your approach or attitude as you faced that situation. When I was a young baseball player, I always made sure my bicycle route through town to the ballpark took me down Hope Street because I thought doing that little ritual would bring my team (and especially me) good luck that night. My Christian hope is deeper than that, because I trust God to have the long view and my journey in hand, to care for me and give me strength, no matter how bleak things seem in the moment. Pray with the children for ways we all need hope.

Musical Suggestions [LH]

Live Into Hope—PH 332

Jesus' Hands Were Kind Hands—UMH 273

O Christ, the Healer—CH 503

When the Poor Ones (Cuando el Pobre)—BP 154

Give Me Jesus—SZ 165

Sister Christine Vladimiroff, O.S.B.

Twenty-Fourth Sunday in Ordinary Time

RCL: Proverbs 1:20-33; Psalm 19; James 3:1-12; Mark 8:27-38

LM: Isaiah 50:4c-9a; Psalm 116:1-2, 3-4, 5-6, 8-9; James 2:14-18; Mark 8:27-35

In today's gospel we enter a world of conflict and suspense, a world of surprising reversals and strange ironies. Jesus' first question is easily answered: "Who do people say that I am?" The disciples simply repeat the stock answers of what they have heard. The second question: "Who do you say that I am?" requires a declaration that is personal to each of us who responds. How would I answer that today? Would I do any better than the disciples, who, in spite of miracles, continue to grapple with Jesus' mystery and mission?

After "leaving all," the disciples have seen Jesus' power in the miracles and have heard him explain the parables and riddles. But they still have difficulty because they lack understanding and are fearful. They do not see the full possibilities of God's rule. The disciples are thinking in human terms and have not grasped the mindset of faith. The call to discipleship is a call to a personal relationship with Jesus, and that relationship comes with demands. Discipleship is about giving up control over one's life and following in trust.

With Peter's answer, "You are the Messiah" (v. 29), the disciples are relieved. They see themselves with Jesus triumphantly marching into Jerusalem, with power and honor following them. Jesus quickly shatters this image as he tries to open the disciples' eyes and hearts to the reality that persecution and death, not privilege and status, may be a

167

consequence of following him. They reject that scenario, and Peter cautions Jesus to move away from such talk.

The picture of the disciples in today's gospel is a touchingly human one, giving us some comfort as we struggle with our own journeys of discipleship. To be truthful, we sometimes select the easy passages of Scripture to inspire us, and we like to hear the reward that will be ours. Today we stand with the disciples and learn that we have chosen a difficult and arduous path.

Jesus is clear. If I want to come after him, I must deny myself—renounce all claims on my life so that it no longer belongs to me. It means being willing to accept Christ's claim, to be totally at the disposition of the work of bringing God's rule to our time and world. As a disciple, I must take up my cross to give myself in the service of others. This compels me to embrace life as a journey moving from self-centeredness to God-centeredness, requiring renunciation and sacrifice. There is no part of my life that my decision to follow Christ does not touch.

As a citizen, I must raise my voice on behalf of those whom society barely notices. I must speak the wisdom of the Gospel as our leaders make laws that keep people hungry or without shelter. As today's reading from Proverbs describes (1:20-21), I too must cry out in the streets, at congressional hearings, at public meetings on local issues that affect poor and hungry people. If I know who Jesus is, I will be confident in my ability to make a difference in the time and world I inhabit.

Jesus is the teacher leading us to explore the paradoxes of Gospel living. We can save our life by losing it. The wisdom of the Cross and not conventional wisdom is what we hear in today's gospel. The challenge of discipleship will make sense only to someone who is willing to leave all and follow Christ. "Who do you say I am?" is the question each of us needs to answer on our journey to God. Our answers will reflect our faith and trust in the God who has called us and toward whom we journey.

Children's Time [LH]

Two avenues present themselves today. One would be to model the way Jesus interacts with his disciples, asking the children first who their parents or Sunday school teachers say Jesus is, and then who they say Jesus is. This may not work well with very young children, but if you have some insightful older ones, you might get some interesting answers. Affirm that each of us experiences Jesus differently and that Jesus wants each of us to know him in our own way. Another fun thing, if the Proverbs passage is read in worship, is to have everyone, adults included, practice shouting out in the same way Wisdom does in the streets and squares. Choose some phrases we'd like to shout in joy as people of faith, such as "God is good . . . All the time" or "Hallelujah . . . Praise the Lord!" Make it a holy uproar!

Musical Suggestions [LH]

Take My Life That It May Be—PSH 289

"Take Up Your Cross," the Savior Said—LBW 398

Lord, Speak to Me—UMH 463

Gifts That Last—GC 583

O Wisdom, Breathed from God—NCH 740

Sister Christine Vladimiroff, O.S.B.

Twenty-Fifth Sunday in Ordinary Time

RCL: Proverbs 31:10-31; Psalm 1; James 3:13–4:3, 7-8a; Mark 9:30-37
LM: Wisdom 2:12, 17-20; Psalm 54:3-4, 5, 6-8; James 3:16–4:3;
   Mark 9:30-37

The Galilean journey in today's gospel is a quiet time away from the crowds, where Jesus can teach his disciples. The disciples have heard the stories and witnessed the miracles. Yet they continue to struggle with the real significance of the teachings. Earlier, when Jesus mentioned his having to suffer and die, they were afraid. So they do not probe Jesus with questions when he repeats the prediction. They really do not want to know the full meaning and what it will do to their lives.

Jesus' time away with his disciples demonstrates his love for them. It is an unhurried time not only to come to greater understanding but also to foster in them the love they need to have for one another and the courage they will need to follow Christ. Discipleship is a relationship, and relationships grow over time and deepen with conversation. They call us to our best selves and make possible feats of courage if we are open to the converting power of love. The gospel recounts a retreat time for the community of the Twelve with Jesus, an opportunity for deeper reflection and probing conversation and challenge.

Jesus again speaks about being handed over, and a mixture of misunderstanding and fear fills the disciples. Along the way they engage in a conversation among themselves about who is the greatest. Jesus is patient with those who left all to follow him. He enters into the private conversation the Twelve are having, but he suggests quite different criteria for greatness. He gives them and us an important lesson—the nature of true Christian greatness. It builds on the Gospel reversals they have heard before.

Jesus is clear that in the community of disciples at that time and now, the first is the last and the servant of all. There is no sophisticated philosophical argument, just a statement that stands in stark contrast to what our world esteems. Hearing it today is no less shocking than when the Twelve heard it for the first time. There is no room for empty ambition or jealousy among Jesus' followers. There is no competition to lord it over others; rather, the competition is to serve others.

Jesus provides a dramatic illustration so that none of the teaching's power is lost. Placing a child in the midst of the Twelve, he puts his arms around the child and invites the disciples to measure their greatness against that of a child. A child is not concerned about being the greatest or first or getting credit for actions. The child is an image and a statement of how the least can indeed be the greatest. I imagine that the picture of Jesus with his arms around the child caused a great deal of discomfort when the disciples considered their earlier conversation about who was the greatest. Yet Jesus offers an even more powerful insight: whoever welcomes the child, the seemingly insignificant and powerless, welcomes Jesus and the One who sent him. When in Jesus' name we welcome children and poor people and those to whom the world's standards assign the least value, we experience Christ's presence. Should we not seek opportunities to put Jesus' words into practice?

As Christians who hear today's gospel, we must live our lives differently. Our actions must proclaim that we put great value on the very things our world sometimes deems worthless. We make our choice for those who are poor not only in the charity we offer but in our struggle to bring about a just and peaceful world. Knowing hungry and poor people teaches us that today's world is not a good place for them to live in. We must offer hope to those who have been denied hope, raising our voices on behalf of those whose voice is not heard. We must embrace them as Jesus did the little child.

For me, the power of today's gospel is what it calls us to as a Church. How do we live our life as a worshiping community differently because we hear Jesus' words not only with our ears but also with our hearts? How do we live and build community by our willingness to be last and to serve others? How does the Church embrace the gospel's wisdom and stand apart from the world's wisdom, which would have us striving to be first, best, and greatest?

Children's Time [LH]

Simply tell the children that Jesus loved the young ones around him. No story in Scripture portrays that more movingly than today's gospel passage, which in one sense contrasts the lust for power with the simplicity of a child's heart. But perhaps today, when you gather the children, speak more to the adults, asking them to think about the ways they seek to be first and how the children there before them offer something that Jesus affirmed as different and vital for our faith. Invite the children to join you in a simple prayer for the adults in the congregation, that they might be servants of all those who are needy, hungry, sick, and poor in our world.

Musical Suggestions [LH]

The Church of Christ in Every Age—PH 421

What Does the Lord Require—UMH 441

Lord, Whose Love Through Humble Service—CH 461

Children of God—NCH 533

Sister Christine Vladimiroff, O.S.B.

Twenty-Sixth Sunday in Ordinary Time

RCL: Esther 7:1-6, 9-10; 9:20-22; Psalm 124; James 5:13-20;
  Mark 9:38-50
LM: Numbers 11:25-29; Psalm 19:8, 10, 12-13, 14; James 5:1-6;
  Mark 9:38-43, 45, 47-48

Being a disciple is not easy, as Jesus' words in today's gospel remind us. The gospel's logic turns our world upside down. We are first if we are last. We lead if we serve. The child is the greatest, and if we welcome the child, we welcome Jesus and the One who sent him.

Yet our responsibility is even more involved as we touch the lives of others. We gain the kingdom when we give a drink in Jesus' name. A simple act of kindness merits the bounty of God's love as a reward. If we lead others away from God, we hear the finality of judgment pronounced against us. The millstone, which was used for grinding grain, was a familiar image to Jesus' hearers, so it brought vivid pictures to their minds. A millstone would plunge a person to the very depths of the sea, swallowing them up, and no effort would free them. Finality!

In today's teaching there is no room for a mediocre attempt at holiness. If we say or do anything to lead a person away from God, we forfeit our vocation as disciple. Said in the positive, we are called to sanctity and to lead others to that same holiness. There is not a lot of room for negotiation. Jesus' hyperbole of cutting off a hand or a foot so as to be able to enter into the kingdom is meant to convey the absolute seriousness of our mission.

This section of Scripture brings back to me a quote of Thomas Merton: "We are supposed to be the light of the world. We are supposed to be a light to ourselves and to others. That may well be what accounts for the fact that the world is in darkness!"[1] Both Jesus and Merton ask us to look around at our world and see that who we are and what we do matter. We have the capacity to be a force for good or evil. If we do not like what we see around us, we need to look to ourselves and pray for the ability to respond in new ways to God's invitation to discipleship.

We have the same struggle as the disciples—living on God's terms or living on human terms. We settle in most instances for being "reasonable" Christians. We go through life marked neither by great holiness nor by profound sinfulness, and thus we keep a certain peace of mind. That was not Jesus' intent in today's gospel. He wants to disturb us, to show us there is no compromise if we are true to our Christian vocation.

We need a certain marginality to live as Jesus' disciples. We need the company of others to help us see the reversal of the world's values; otherwise we may succumb to valuing honor as identity, power as privilege, wealth as blessing, and security as salvation. Christians hold an alternative vision that cherishes service as noble and honorable, sharing our goods as justice in God's plan, casting our lot with poor people as a certain step toward salvation.

Still, we are too reluctant to bring the searing vision of God's rule to the fore as our world moves toward war. We are too cautious to suggest a radical change in the economy so that children will not be hungry and women will have adequate shelter. We are too subtle as we decry the violence of capital punishment. As Jesus' followers, we cannot look dispassionately at the evil around us and assume that we can continue living our life as before. Jesus' words to us today are uncompromising but full of hope. "Everyone will be salted with fire" (9:49). Today let us as disciples touch that fire and live in peace as we pursue God's rule on earth.

Children's Time [LH]

Count how many "communities" the children live in: church, family, school, town or city, state, nation, world, universe . . . others? Re-

---

1. Thomas Merton, *Life and Holiness* (Garden City, N.Y.: Image Books, 1964) 16.

mind them that they are an important part of all those communities and that being in community means we care for one another. Talk about the ways we do this: helping those who are sick or weak, inviting others to join the community and offer their talents, celebrating together, meeting to talk about problems and conflicts, asking our leaders to take action to resolve community issues. We can't live without these relationships in community, because they help us share our life with God in the world around us.

Musical Suggestions [LH]

Blessed Jesus, at Your Word—PH 454

When the Church of Jesus—UMH 592

Christ Loves the Church—UMH 590

Shake Up the Morning—GC 529

Sois la Semilla (You Are the Seed)—NCH 528

You Are Salt for the Earth, O People—NCH 181

Sister Christine Vladimiroff, O.S.B.

Twenty-Seventh Sunday in Ordinary Time

RCL: Job 1:1; 2:1-10; Psalm 26; Hebrews 1:1-4; 2:5-12; Mark 10:2-16
LM: Genesis 2:18-24; Psalm 128:1-2, 3, 4-5, 6; Hebrews 2:9-11;
  Mark 10:2-16 or 10:2-12

In today's gospel the disciples again struggle to live in terms of God's rule and not the earthly wisdom of their times. The picture of Jesus with the children has often been romanticized in bad religious art, and so we forget the message. Jesus insists that the kingdom of God belongs to the children. What is more, our very entrance into the kingdom depends on our being like the child: "Whoever does not receive the kingdom of God as a little child will never enter it" (10:15). Jesus builds on the message he gave the disciples earlier when he challenged their ideal of greatness by putting his arm around a child. The disciples have forgotten that lesson and are now rebuking people who bring their children for Jesus to touch. Those closest to Jesus are too focused on their proximity to him and on their own ideal of importance to care about the children.

In his second inaugural address in 1937, President Franklin Delano Roosevelt said, "The test of our progress is not whether we add more to the abundance of those who have much; it is whether we provide enough for those who have too little."[1] No doubt human infants and children are vulnerable and often are among those with "too little."

1. John Bartlett, *Familiar Quotations,* 13th ed., ed. Christopher Morley (Boston: Little, Brown, 1955) 919.

Unlike other species, children are completely dependent on the adults of the family and community that surround them. They learn how to love because they are loved. They learn trust because significant adults do not abandon them. They learn language because they hear it around them and it is spoken to them. They walk because we give them our hand and hold it tightly during the first few, unsure steps. They emerge as unique human beings mediated through the social interaction in family and in community. We also know the tragic outcomes of children who grow up in a world that is hostile and uncaring. We reap the resulting hate and violence in our communities.

In what way can we fashion a world in which people can live together in peace? What can I change so that every child has enough food to grow strong, enough education to open the mind to a world of wonder, and enough love to fill the soul with the capacity to bond with others? We who hear this gospel must become engaged in the political, economic, and social debates of our times. Economic and political structures can be oppressive or liberating. Foreign policy legislation can enable an equitable sharing of resources or cause famine to go unaddressed. Society's attitudes and behavior can open our frontiers to immigrants, providing them with new opportunities for life, or society can further marginalize them and increase their isolation and poverty. Our actions are how we embrace the world and bless it as Jesus did the children who surrounded him.

This childlike quality is what Jesus says makes a person eligible for the kingdom. It is not the innocence of an untested childhood that we need to recover; it is the capacity to live in the world confident that what we need and will need come as gift from God. It is the power to stake our lives on the promise that God has made—nothing else is of value. There is no room for discussion about being the greatest if you know at the level of your soul that all you have comes as blessing from God's hand. Your very existence is gift and blessing.

The kingdom demands this radical dependence that Jesus describes in the image of a child in today's Scripture. This is a dependence that makes us open to receive from others, to learn new ways, to change what we value, and to receive all as gift. We are challenged to accept God's kingdom like a child and learn the ways of that kingdom, embarking on a process, a developmental journey, much as a child learns to become an adult. It takes a lifetime to learn the gospel's upside-down logic. What is at stake is the kingdom.

Children's Time [LH]

From newspapers, magazines, Bread for the World resources, the Children's Defense Fund website, or other places, find pictures of children—lots of different children. Invite each of the children in your group to take a picture and look at the child's face. Remind them that these pictured children come from many places around the world. Ask them if God loves the child whose picture they have. Then have them look at each other and ask the same question. Assure them that Jesus had a special place for children, a place close to him. Finish by inviting the congregation to join in singing "Jesus loves the little children."

Musical Suggestions [LH]

Hope for the Children—BP 90

Precious Lord, Take My Hand—SZ 179

Great Work Has God Begun in You—NCH 353

O God, We Bear the Imprint of Your Face—NCH 585

Cureton L. Johnson

Twenty-Eighth Sunday in Ordinary Time

RCL: Job 23:1-9, 16-17; Psalm 22:1-15; Hebrews 4:12-16; Mark 10:17-31
LM: Wisdom 7:7-11; Psalm 90:12-13, 14-15, 16-17; Hebrews 4:12-13;
    Mark 10:17-30 or 10:17-27

A minister was leading a spiritual discussion with a group of inner-city men and women infected with HIV when the conversation turned to the first two chapters of Genesis. Many participants found hope from learning that they were "made in the image of God" with a capacity to communicate with the Divine.

In spite of all the positive feedback, one weary-looking soul found no solace. This man's eyes were reddened, and his countenance was beaten by his medical problems. Sadly, he was convinced that hell loomed as his unalterable destination and no power could deliver him.

Now just imagine Job's predicament. In a matter of minutes he loses wealth, children, and health. Here is an upright, righteous man who does not deserve his calamities. Hence Job feels that God has abandoned him and unjustly thrust him into a hell of severe suffering. As a result, he has bitter complaints against God and seeks God's dwelling place to present arguments for his innocence. Surely the Almighty Judge of heaven and earth will give heed to his case and bring relief.

But Job cannot find God, who now appears distant and inaccessible. To Job, "thick clouds enwrap [God], so that he does not see, and he walks on the dome [highest part] of heaven" (Job 22:14). Job's heart faints under the terror of his situation. How many desperate people turn to suicide as a way out of such pain, feeling that only the "thick darkness"

179

of death can relieve their grief? Job refuses to be silent amidst his terror. At the vortex of his testing, he will not let gloom overwhelm him.

Indeed, God expects us to seek and inquire of him in all aspects of our lives (Prov 3:5, 6), and especially when we are in the depths of despair. As difficult as this may be, we need to know that the Lord is near, to hear the wisdom that only God can provide.

In the Roman Catholic reading from Wisdom, King Solomon seeks wisdom and is blessed as he prays to and pleads with the Creator. He acknowledges God's wisdom and calls the Creator's answers to his prayers better than his riches. But can poor, hungry, oppressed, and disease-disrupted people be blessed like Solomon?

When hurting, poor people enter your church, do they find God there in your congregation? How many homeless and hungry people, how many gays and lesbians, unemployed and unemployable people find God there? How many single parents, unwed mothers and fathers, pimps and prostitutes can find God in your house of worship? One preacher has said that the Church should "go to hell," meaning the Church should go into the "hell holes" of the world to rescue people who are dying and perishing.

Have U.S. churches become country clubs for those who seek "prosperity religion" and are concerned only about their health and wealth? Do modern Christians shun touching the "untouchables"? Could the beaten-down man with AIDS find God in such places? Does today's passage from Mark's Gospel challenge us to ask if we worship our wealth more than we worship the Savior we say we follow?

Most people with HIV/AIDS don't have the resources of sports stars, entertainers, and celebrities. Many are scorned and ridiculed inside and outside our churches. Like Job, they are terrified. Does God heed their cry?

The preacher/author of the letter to the Hebrews, writing in times of persecution, assures Christians that "no creature is hidden, but all are naked and laid bare to the eyes of the one to whom we must render an account" (4:13). Indeed, "we do not have a high priest who is unable to sympathize with our weaknesses; but we have one who in every respect has been tested as we are" (4:15). Christ Jesus was truly innocent and sinless, yet he was tested on a cruel Roman cross. God's wisdom and faithfulness that supported Christ in his suffering are the same resources available to us. They are mobile enough to reach all people in all situations.

So all can "approach the throne of grace with boldness" (4:16), where Christ Jesus will heed our case. He will hear our arguments, consider our complaints, and intercede for us before the Creator in heaven.

In the wilderness of abandonment, one may curse God and die or seek God and live! Oh, that we may hear the "still small voice" of God beckoning us onward and "receive mercy and find grace to help in time of need" (4:16).

Children's Time [LH]

Ask the children whether they think God ever goes on vacation. The Bible assures us that God always cares, every moment of our lives. There are no times when God is too busy to take notice of us. Well, then, are there times when God just notices certain types of people, such as only rich people or famous people, or just adults and not children? No, God has a special way of caring for people who need help—people who don't have enough food, or have lost all they had, or are very sad. We can trust God to care deeply for us, whoever we are and whatever happens to us.

Musical Suggestions

Soon-a Will Be Done—AAH 587

I Love the Lord, He Heard My Cry—AAH 395 (gospel); 394 (old metered style)

Rescue the Perishing—NB 142

The Solid Rock—NB 223

Cureton L. Johnson

Twenty-Ninth Sunday in Ordinary Time

RCL: Job 38:1-7 (34-41); Psalm 104:1-9, 24, 35c; Hebrews 5:1-10;
Mark 10:35-45

LM: Isaiah 53:10-11; Psalm 33:4-5, 18-19, 20, 22; Hebrews: 4:14-16;
Mark 10:35-45 or 10:42-45

What, be a slave? Can't you hear the protests? As the spiritual says, "Before I'd be a slave, I'll be buried in my grave." But in Mark 10, Jesus tells his disciples, "Whoever wishes to become great among you must be your servant, and whoever wishes to be first among you must be slave of all" (v. 43).

A slave is the property of another and under someone else's domination. Such was the evil system in fifteen states during the pre-Civil War period. But Jesus' slave/servant model bears no resemblance to that wickedness. Christ calls his disciples to be slave/servants of goodness and godliness, to be God's property in a fallen world.

James and John are two pathetically slow-maturing disciples, shackled by the chains of sinful ambition. Their mother, Zebedee's wife, has a hand in this corruption as they envision Jesus coming into his glory and finally overcoming the Roman tyrants in their homeland (Matt

20:20). But Jesus puts a stop to their nonsense, saying that they must put *others* first and be slaves to *others* to rise in God's kingdom.

"To rise, by any means, is wonderfully American," according to Randall Robinson's critical writings about U.S. social culture in *The Reckoning*.[1] "To lift" [others], he says, "is a loser's obsession." Look at how Enron and WorldCom corporate leaders used deceptive accounting practices to "rise" in the markets. Observe how the CEOs and boards of large U.S. drug companies denied HIV/AIDS medications to poor nations of the world. Visualize inner-city check-cashing rackets that extract high fees and prey upon poor people, and opportunist lenders who devour minority homeowners with savage mortgage-refinancing schemes that balloon and burst hard-working people's American dream. The prophet Amos still cries out, "Let justice roll down like waters" (5:24).

Whatever happened to slave/servant leaders like Martin Luther King Jr., like Fannie Lou Hamer of Mississippi, and Rosa Parks? Where are the servants like Quaker rancher and sanctuary-movement activist Jim Corbett or the Church's servant to poor people, Mother Teresa? They fought for freedom and put their lives on the line to serve others. They refused to be slaves to evil or to serve the demons of injustice and oppression but were willing to be slaves for the one God of justice and righteousness and mercy.

Jesus tells his two ambitious disciples, "You do not know what you are asking" (10:38). Were they able to drink his cup of suffering and sorrows? Would they be willing to undergo the fiery "baptism" he would undergo at Calvary? Yet only those willing to disregard personal comforts and willing to suffer with Jesus for others are truly free. Indeed, Jesus clearly became a "slave" for us by giving his life as a "ransom for many" (v. 45).

This kind of slavery produces freedom in us and in others. Ched Myers, in *Binding the Strong Man*, notes that "leadership belongs only to those who learn and follow the way of nonviolence—who are 'prepared' not to dominate but to serve and suffer at Jesus' side. . . . the way of 'servanthood' has been transformed by the Human One into the way of liberation."[2]

1. Randall Robinson, *The Reckoning: What Blacks Owe to Each Other* (New York: The Penguin Group, 2002) 108.
2. Ched Myers, *Binding the Strong Man: A Political Reading of Mark's Story of Jesus* (Maryknoll, N.Y.: Orbis Books, 1988) 278, 279.

Our inner cities and rural communities cry out for people of all races to leave their comforts and to serve as slaves alongside Christ and suffering people. Walk with Christ in bringing aid and encouragement on street corners, in Appalachian hills, and in the "hood." If Christian disciples want seats of prestige in God's kingdom, those seats are located wherever people suffer from drug and substance abuse, from domestic violence, from loneliness and hopelessness. This is the Church's mission: to serve others and show them the good news of liberation in Christ. We are to "let the oppressed go free" (Luke 4:18). Bound with Christ in servanthood, we are free to challenge the demonic forces that breed hatred and malice and arrogance and callousness in the world and to speak out against injustice and greed.

One day there will be a new heaven and a new earth. Then we who learned to be Christ's slave/servants as James and John did will share with him in the rule and operations of that permanent and eternal kingdom of God. We'll hear him say, "Well done, good and faithful servants." In that great day the First World will become the Third, and the Third World will become the First. Amen!

Children's Time [LH]

Tell the children you're going for a walk and you want them to follow you. Ask who wants to be first! Chances are many hands will go up. Then ask who wants to be last. Many fewer hands are likely. Say that's exactly what Jesus and his disciples are talking about in today's Scripture. We usually think it's best to be first, to have lots of power, to get ahead. That's what James and John want. Almost nobody likes to be last. But Jesus says it's different if you're one of his flock. We need to serve each other, to let ourselves come last sometimes so that we can help other people and not always try to get ahead of others. It's not easy, but it's Jesus' way. Pray that God will give us ways to serve and be happy in being last.

Musical Suggestions

Anthem: Lord, Make Me an Instrument of Thy Peace

Oh, Freedom—AAH 545

"Are Ye Able," Said the Master—NB 270

Cureton L. Johnson

Thirtieth Sunday in Ordinary Time

RCL: Job 42:1-6, 10-17; Psalm 34:1-8 (19-22); Hebrews 7:23-28;
Mark 10:46-52

LM: Jeremiah 31:7-9; Psalm 126:1-2, 2-3, 4-5, 6; Hebrews 5:1-6;
Mark 10:46-52

Psalm 34 is like a pineapple upside-down cake. The best part—the pineapple slices, brown sugar, butter, maraschino cherries, and walnuts—go into the cooking pan first and simmer into the cake batter poured on top. After baking, the cake is turned right side up, and the fruit mix flavors the whole cake.

Similarly, the psalmist pours out blessings, adoration, praises, and gratitude to God in the first eight verses of this thanksgiving hymn. A joyful "fruit of praise" precedes a brief explanation (v. 4) for such enthusiasm. The Creator's life-giving power and deliverance inspire praise and glory and boasting. Such enthusiasm for God saturates the psalmist's heart and freely flows forth from his or her mouth. Such faith invites others to taste for themselves the Lord's goodness (v. 8).

The "fruit of praise" also comes from the mouth of a destitute blind beggar named Bartimaeus, who in Mark 10 boldly calls out, "Son of David, have mercy on me" (v. 47). The surrounding crowd tries to quiet the boisterous man, but he is not deterred. Without natural eyesight, he sees what others cannot—the Messiah! When Jesus beckons him, Bartimaeus throws off his cloak—one of the poor beggar's few possessions—and springs up to Jesus, saying, "Teacher" or "my master" (from Rabbouni, a heightened form of Rabbi).[1] Such positive expectations and praise are forces for liberation when we lovingly offer them to God.

Very often poor minority students are the objects of low expectations in our schools. Many teachers and parents estimate potential based on wealth and background. Yet "the most important factor in student performance is not parent demography or how much money the school has, but teacher/parent expectations," according to educational consultant Jawanza Kunjufu.[2] He advises adults to give five parts of praise for every one part of criticism and to expect great things from all children. Let them know that you believe in them!

Even the Lord invites praise and high expectations. In the Roman Catholic reading, no one expects much of Jeremiah when he is so crazy as to predict Jerusalem's destruction. He finds great strongholds of resistance in his time and suffers terribly for his faithfulness. Yet Jeremiah speaks boldly until even he receives a "fruit of praise" report from heaven, an announcement of Israel's restoration to its homeland: "Shout with joy for Jacob . . . proclaim your praise . . . the Lord has delivered his people" (31:7). This pre-restoration oracle includes exiled blind and lame people, mothers and pregnant women (31:8). No one is left behind, no matter how vulnerable or marginalized.

The psalmist touches the same chord: "Let the humble hear and be glad" (Ps 34:2). Those who are humble, oppressed, afflicted, and poor, and even the children who aren't expected to be much, are all invited to hear the psalmist's praises and join the gladness! The wonderful taste of "life" from God is available to all!

Then watch the Lord begin to deliver you from "all" your fears. Expectant praise helps deconstruct and put down the evil and false gods that invade life. Praise dismantles negative forces before they bring us to our knees. Praise breathes life and health and strength! Don't wait for Sunday to get your praise on, but "taste and see that the Lord is good" every day!

Sometimes, like Job, we struggle through a bevy of problems, but God responds. We take a step toward God, and we find that the Creator has been stepping toward us all along! Exalting the Lord's name often evokes God's blessings.

1. Douglas R. A. Hare, *Mark* (Louisville: Westminster/John Knox Press, 1996) 132.
2. Jawanza Kunjufu, *Developing Positive Self-Images and Discipline in Black Children* (Chicago: American Images, 1984) 50.

Hebrews 7 assures us that Jesus Christ is our advocate, available to us 24/7 and continually speaking for us in God's presence. Christ receives our "fruit of praise" up in glory and responds to our joyful expectations. Christ is the first fruits of our salvation (1 Cor 15:20) and thereby saturates us with eternal "life and spirit" from above. Like the pineapples and brown sugar, he sweetens our lives in an upside-down kind of world.

Don't allow the world to deny you a "fruit of praise" dessert. So skip the main course sometimes—you can come back to that. Eat the dessert! Cut to the chase! Have some cherries jubilee, some double chocolate fudge, some pie a la mode, some pineapple upside-down cake! Come and rave and boast and clamor about the goodness of the Lord. Come magnify the Lord and exalt his name together! O taste the Lord firsthand! Enjoy a personal and corporate experience with God's goodness!

Children's Time [LH]

Bring in some seasonal treat that is both attractive-looking and good to eat. Invite the children to admire what it looks like, and then taste a bit of it. Exclaim how good it is and how beautiful. Point out that Psalm 34 asks us to "taste and see that the Lord is good." Ask if they've ever seen God or tasted God? Of course not. But God's goodness is so real that we can almost taste it. God gave us the good and tasty things we eat, and the beauty of the mountains and the ocean, of our own streets and homes, and of the people around us. We can "taste and see" that God is good by looking around and realizing that God's creation is very good. Offer the children another taste of what you brought as you thank God for all that's tasty in our world.

Musical Suggestions

Total Praise (from Psalm 121)—AAH 113

Marguerite Shuster

Thirty-First Sunday in Ordinary Time

RCL: Ruth 1:1-18; Psalm 146; Hebrews 9:11-14; Mark 12:28-34
LM: Deuteronomy 6:2-6; Psalm 18:2-3, 3-4, 47, 51; Hebrews 7:23-28;
   Mark 12:28b-34

We are accustomed to reading the beginning of the book of Ruth as a supreme example of the human love and loyalty of one woman for another. But in doing that, we may overlook the fact that Ruth's profession of devotion to Naomi and Naomi's God results from the utter destitution of widows forced to flee the land in search of food. While Naomi sees what happens to her absolutely in terms of what the Lord gives and withholds, this strong sense of God's sovereign governance in no way makes her passive or saps her human resolve. Surely she knows this God as who the psalm reveals him to be—One who gives food to those who are hungry and shows special care for orphans and widows. But the ultimate divine justice God promises to poor and oppressed people often seems far removed from their current desperate circumstances, circumstances that require human action and responsibility.

We are not likely to think of Naomi as an example of the "neighbor" with a claim to Ruth's love, to whom Jesus refers in the second half of his summary of the Law in Mark's Gospel. (Recall that the summary begins with the Shema of the Deuteronomy text: we will not rightly love our neighbor without first loving God. Apparently Ruth intuitively understands this. She does not suppose she can separate love for Naomi from embracing her God.) After all, not only is Ruth destitute herself, but she knows Naomi, her mother-in-law, very well. Yet therein lies a key lesson: what, indeed, would Ruth have done had she not known Naomi personally? Would she not have assumed quite reasonably that there was no bond between them and that she must, of course, go her own way?

An old Hasidic story tells of a congregation that thinks they have a bright, innovative idea. They decide to put an end to the need for poor people to beg from door to door. The story does not say, but perhaps they see this practice as demeaning, or perhaps they consider it as intrusive as a dinnertime telemarketing call. In any case, they plan instead to put up a box into which the well-to-do can drop their offerings, according to their means, which then will be distributed according to need. A wise rabbi puts an immediate end to this alleged innovation, however, for he sees it for what it is. Hidden just below the surface is the ancient (and also very modern) desire to avoid looking one's needy neighbor in the eye.

Of course, times change, and our world has become stunningly complex. Individual efforts simply do not suffice in the face of structures and policies that institutionalize need. Those who work at the national and international level to combat famine and oppression are essential and require the support of all who care about their neighbors, near and far. The need for action on a large scale can scarcely be overemphasized. But these efforts do not obviate the necessity of the personal. In fact, it may well be that removing our giving too fully from the context of immediate human interaction is one of the things that turn our sacrifices into the "dead works" that our text from Hebrews decries. We get to feel good about ourselves by giving simply money, without either the joy or the pain of meeting need face to face. But "feeling good about ourselves" threatens to become precisely the futile attempt at self-justification from which Jesus gave his life to deliver us.

God came to us in person and gave himself in person because all the long centuries of action at a distance, of sending others to tell of his purposes and to implore justice and righteousness, were not enough. They still aren't. We do not have to repeat what Jesus has done once and for all. We do not have to count the adequacy of our means, for however great they may be, they are surely inadequate to the stunning needs before us. But we do need to attend, personally, to the neighbors Jesus has given us to get to know and to love. When we engage in that personal knowing and loving, we cannot escape seeing the pressing need for larger-scale efforts as well.

Children's Time [MM]

You might make and hold up a poster with a heart on it. Explain that today we're going to talk about love (based on the two great commandments in Mark 12). First, ask the children how God shows love for people. Enjoy their answers. Ask how we show our love for God. Then ask how other people show their love for us. Finally, ask how they show love to others. They might well be "loved out" by the time you finish! Help them see that all love flows out of God's love for us.

Musical Suggestions [LH]

The Gift of Love—CH 526

Blest Be the Dear Uniting Love—UMH 566

Brothers and Sisters of Mine Are the Hungry—BP 148

Un mandamiento nuevo—NCH 389

Covenant Hymn—GC 797

Come, Let Us Walk This Road Together—BP 160

Wherever You Go—GC 867

Marguerite Shuster

Thirty-Second Sunday in Ordinary Time

RCL: Ruth 3:1-5; 4:13-17; Psalm 127; Hebrews 9:24-28; Mark 12:38-44
LM: 1 Kings 17:10-16; Psalm 146:7, 8-9, 9-10; Hebrews 9:24-28;
    Mark 12:38-44 or 12:41-44

The generosity of those who are truly poor, like the grasping, cling-
ing anxiety of the very rich, is legendary. This reality is reflected both
in today's gospel lesson, often referred to as "the widow's mite," and
in the story of the widow of Zarephath in 1 Kings. Here are people
who truly have nothing and yet are willing to give the very last of their
resources. The starving widow of Zarephath, it is true, acts on the
strength of the prophet Elijah's fantastic promise about the Lord's
provision (would we be willing to rely ahead of time on such a promise? *Should* we?). The widow at the Temple treasury apparently acts
simply out of a sense of the rightness of giving and not holding back.
The text puts a curious emphasis on her two coins. Why doesn't she
just keep one of the coins, knowing that she's still showing extraordinary generosity on a percentage basis? Yet she throws in both. Does
she have in mind texts like Psalm 146, full of hope for those in extreme
need? We do not know, and yet we see the trusting openness of her
heart and hand.

One of the few observations I still remember from sermons I heard
in childhood came from a sermon on the widow's mite. The preacher
commented—as have, no doubt, many before and after him—that the
size of a gift is to be measured, not by its numerical size, but by what

the giver has left for herself. That comment not only stuck in my conscience but came back to me in force when, decades ago now, I made
a pastoral call on a visitor to the congregation I then served, a very rich
man who knew that he would shortly die of pancreatic cancer. He had
few heirs or obligations of any kind, as I recall. However, he spoke of
his difficulty making a commitment to the church, for he knew his financial involvement had to be part of the package (though I had mentioned nothing of such matters). With the utter, unselfconscious
naïveté of one who obviously had no conception of what it is like to be
poor and to lack enough resources to obtain essentials, he said he
thought it would be easier to tithe if one were poor, because then not
so much money would be involved. He could see only the numbers.
He seemed to be wholly unaware that he could give away 90 percent
of his wealth and still have a great deal more than enough.

Perhaps the very rich, whether individuals or nations, often find no
heart for giving because they truly do not understand and lack a gift of
imaginative empathy. Generosity that goes beyond the easy and per-
functory surely requires something we can only call heart. Fear of death
and even lurking suspicions of impending judgment, judgment alluded
to in the text from Hebrews, are obviously not enough, as the story of
the cancer patient makes clear. Not that the rich are automatically hardhearted, of course. Boaz, who befriends and then marries Ruth, is rich,
yet he treats her with attentive kindness from the time he first sees her
scavenging for food on his property. The warmth with which he follows the teaching that one must not take everything from the field but
must leave something for gleaners provides something of a model for
those of us inclined to be resentful of taxes and undiscerning of the
good uses to which they can and should be put. It has never been the
case that we have an absolute right to all we produce; we always have a
deep responsibility to see to the welfare of others. Now, we have opportunity to do so in part through the workings of government, but with
the sharp caveat that we must insist that government protect not just
our profits but most especially those who cannot protect themselves.

In the case of Boaz and Ruth, the Lord not only blessed their union
with offspring (note Psalm 127) but also chose that Jesus himself should
be born of their lineage, that of a rich Israelite wed to a poor foreigner.
Indeed, the Lord is no respecter of persons. For oppressed people,
physical need seems to promote their having generous hearts toward
others. For many of the rest of us, I suspect tender hearts may come as

we acknowledge our own desperate need as sinners—need that no human can satisfy on his or her own—and as we gratefully receive what the Lord, by his own self-sacrifice, has done on our behalf (Heb 9:26).

Children's Time [MM]

Tell the children about the beautifully fresh water of the American Great Lakes (or a nearby clean lake or river). Contrast that by telling about the virtually dead Great Salt Lake in Utah (or a nearby source of stagnant water). Explain the difference: where the water flows through, it is renewed and cleansed; where the water stays in the same place, it becomes undrinkable. People are the same way! When God's blessings flow through us, we experience spiritual health. When we keep God's blessings to ourselves, we become spiritually polluted. That's why it's healthy to give our money, our food, all we have to others. Nothing is more clean and beautiful than Jesus, who let everything flow through himself for us (Phil 2:7). By the way, you can make this message more vivid if you collect and show water from a nearby "clean" source and a stagnant source as well.

Musical Suggestions [LH]

What Gift Can We Bring—UMH 87

'Tis the Gift to Be Simple (Simple Gifts)—BP 167

You Made Your Human Family One—BP 119

God, Whose Giving Knows No Ending—NCH 565

Marguerite Shuster

Thirty-Third Sunday in Ordinary Time

RCL: 1 Samuel 1:4-20; 1 Samuel 2:1-10; Hebrews 10:11-14 (15-18)
    19-25; Mark 13:1-8

LM: Daniel 12:1-3; Psalm 16:5, 8, 9-10, 11; Hebrews 10:11-14, 18;
    Mark 13:24-32

Most of today's readings deal explicitly or implicitly with the certainty of judgment to come. The striking reversals of Hannah's song in 1 Samuel 2 are the marks of this judgment. Those who are hungry, barren, and feeble will at last have their needs supplied, while the seemingly secure and all those whom the Lord counts his enemies will be brought low (see also Heb 10:13). Does the Temple look large and strong? Even it shall fall (Mark 13:2). Have some lived out their lives and died without seeing justice done? They shall yet know justice in another life, if not in this one (Dan 12:2).

Just because the end time is unknown and seems to tarry long, we dare not deceive ourselves, for it will surely come. Or if spiraling natural and political disasters lead many to assert with confidence that the end time is surely just around the corner, we dare not sink back into "observer status," as if effort and endurance and work on behalf of those in need were no longer required. The time of terrible suffering may persist far beyond our imagining, requiring sustained courage from those who would serve God faithfully. All we can say for sure is that in that great Day, neither the living nor the dead will escape the searching light of God's sure knowledge.

But we must not think that we can wait until things are at last evened out by divine fiat, especially since our own efforts are so comparatively feeble. Nor may we think that we can safely mock the unfortunate ones, as Peninnah provokes her barren rival (1 Sam 1:6), exulting for as long as we can in the privileged status we may enjoy now. (Does Peninnah suppose, as it is so easy to do, that Hannah's plight is, one way or another, her own fault, so that sympathy and support are scarcely called for? Or is her attitude a defense against the deadly conviction that any increase in Hannah's status means a sure decrease in her own? After all, in a world of limited resources, it is not just paranoia that might lead a person or a nation to think that if someone else gets more, she will surely end up with less.) No, the point, as the text from Hebrews makes plain, is that we who believe in the Lord live in a magnificent hope that makes such competition unnecessary as well as unseemly. What is more, we are to gather together regularly to engage in an altogether different sort of mutual provocation—a provocation to love and to do good deeds, most especially as we anticipate the approaching end. When we meet together for mutual encouragement, especially as we think about the needs and human rights of others, it makes it much harder to fool ourselves about our self-serving attitudes and motives.

As we think about the unfailing justice, and hence the certain reversals, to come, we might ponder one of the old stories Elie Wiesel likes to tell. It seems the famous Rebbe Zusia, visiting an inn somewhere, is mistaken by a wealthy guest for a beggar; the guest, of course, treating him accordingly. Later, learning his true identity, the rich man begs his forgiveness, pleading ignorance. "Why do you ask Zusia to forgive you?" Rebbe Zusia says, shaking his head and smiling. "You haven't done anything bad to him; it is not Zusia you insulted but a poor beggar, so go and ask the beggars, everywhere, to forgive you."[1]

But at the same time we do well to recall Simone Weil's caution that "God is not present, even if we invoke him, where the afflicted are merely regarded as an occasion for doing good."[2] Something far larger than that is required. The Lord who has saved us has given us one an-

---

1. Elie Wiesel, *Souls on Fire: Portraits and Legends of Hasidic Masters*, trans. Marion Wiesel (New York: Summit Books, 1972) 126.
2. Simone Weil, *Waiting for God* (London: Routledge and Kegan Paul, 1951) 91.

other, not as means to our individual ends, but as brothers and sisters to love.

Children's Time [MM]

Tell the story of Peninnah's mocking of Hannah, explaining the shame Hannah experienced because of her barrenness. Point out that this still happens today—children sometimes make fun of others because they lack the right kind of shoes, the right kind of clothes, a large home, or the latest, coolest toys. Help them realize that, as Martin Luther said, "we are beggars. This is true." None of us deserves what we have; everything we have is a gift from God.

Musical Suggestions [LH]

Tell Out, My Soul—UMH 200

My Soul Gives Glory to My God—CH 130

My Heart Is Overflowing (The Song of Hannah)—NCH 15

O Day of God, Draw Nigh—PH 452

Canticle of the Turning—GC 556

Marguerite Shuster

◼

Christ the King

◼

RCL: 2 Samuel 23:1-7; Psalm 132:1-12 (13-18); Revelation 1:4b-8; John 18:33-37

LM: Daniel 7:13-14; Psalm 93:1, 1-2, 5; Revelation 1:5-8; John 18:33b-37

Christ the King—a Sunday when we affirm that even now, in however hidden ways, our Lord rules all the kings of the earth and that one day his rule will be hidden no longer, but every eye will see him (Rev 1:7; see also Dan 7:13-14). The books of Revelation and Daniel both make clear that it is not just over individuals but over "tribes" and "nations" that the Lord holds sway, tribes and nations that must obey and will be called to account for their actions.

The Lord rules the kings of the earth? The Lord holds sway over the maneuverings of heads of state distinguished by nothing so much as their relentless, even vicious pursuit of personal and national interest? If this be "rule," what would letting things go their wildly out of control way look like? Do we not slander Christ to name him king of a world like this one, where so many die of starvation while others threaten their health with ever increasing obesity?

Yet the problem is hardly new with respect to the One we picture as reigning from the cross, the One who comes to us in the first place in the most unprepossessing and unlikely way possible? After all, way back at the beginning, what is Pilate to think of the Jesus who seems so obviously in his complete power? And what is Jesus to say to a ruler who can think of rule only in terms of all the usual machinations, power plays, and exercises of brute force common to those with earthly authority? What can Jesus say but that his kingdom is not from here and is not like the kingdoms Pilate has in mind? And what can Pilate think but that such an answer is devoid of all worldly relevance (and is there any other kind of relevance in Pilate's universe?)?

Yet there is that underlying question of the "truth" to which Jesus testifies, of something that apparently goes deeper than what we see on the surface. Bits of it linger in all of us whose consciences are not seared beyond all retrieval — including, we trust, in those who frame our public policies as well as in those who seek to influence policies that relieve hunger and oppression. Visions of that truth appear in David's words about the just ruler who rules in the fear of God and in the psalmist's picture of the place where the Lord dwells and where poor people are satisfied with bread. We have a sense of what a better world looks like. The very fact that, for the most part, we *know* better than we *do* proves not only that we are sinners but also that, deep down, we recognize righteousness. In that recognition, Christ rules even now.

Christ's rule peeks through when we feel convicted by a cartoon like the old one from the *New Yorker* I have before me, showing three fish of graduated sizes in a line. The first, a little one, mouth closed, concludes, "There is no justice in the world." The middle-sized one, mouth open to devour the little fish, ponders, "There is some justice in the world." And the biggest and last, mouth open wide, thinks confidently, "The world is just." Christ's rule peeks through when we resonate to Thomas Jefferson's remark, "Indeed I tremble for my country when I reflect that God is just." Christ's rule peeks through whenever we are drawn to what is good and pure.

Christ is King. Christ rules *now* in the true, deep-down structure of things. But one day that deep-down structure will, by God's own act, break through to the surface. It will become manifest and shape the whole of reality. And whether we — and, indeed, our nation and the nations of the world — greet the new day with joy or with wailing will depend, not on our guilt quotient or on how many times we have seen the reality of things peek through, but on what we have done with our sins, public and private, and our sinful resistance to that reality. Is the new, wholly just world one we want to live in? Really? If not now, when?

Children's Time [MM]

Ask the children, "If Jesus were the king of this world, what would the world look like?" You may have to prompt them a little. Would there be war with the Prince of Peace reigning? Would there be hunger when Jesus can miraculously produce food? Would there be violence and anger as the king proclaims, "Love one another, as I have loved you." Ask them, "Wouldn't it be great if Jesus were king of this world?" Now comes the twist: Jesus is the king of this world! He is the king of all that is! And if Jesus is the king and he wants us to help rid the world of violence, warfare, and hunger, what are we going to do about it?! We can start right away, helping make the world more the way the king wants it to be!

Musical Suggestions [LH]

Eternal Christ, You Rule—NCH 302

We Hail You God's Anointed—NCH 104

Bring Forth the Kingdom—GC 658

Gather Us In—GC 744

We Are Called—GC 718

Herman Diers

Watch Night/New Year

RCL: Ecclesiastes 3:1-13; Psalm 8; Revelation 21:1-6a; Matthew 25:31-46

Here it is—the premier text for Christians concerned about hunger! It hardly requires exposition, only faithfulness. What is it doing here amidst the revelry of New Year's Eve and the sleepiness of New Year's Day? Actually, there may be no better time, no better context for us to contemplate it.

Tonight's readings suggest three stages of movement and action. Let's explore them.

First, we can think of ourselves on a threshold. This is the time between—no longer the old year and not yet the new. Such times are dangerous ones, when people are vulnerable. Signs in the New York subway warn riders not to ride between the cars because it's dangerous. So is the threshold between the station platform and the subway car.

Life holds lots of these threshold moments—puberty, coming of age, graduation from school, the time between jobs, marriage, and death. Every culture has stories and ceremonies to help its members cross these precarious thresholds—initiations, dances and ordeals, masks and costumes, fasts and gluttonous feasts. Even our "secular" culture has its Halloween and Mardi Gras as well as New Year's.

In the reading from Ecclesiastes, the Teacher in a Hebrew school of thought writes of the alternation of seasons and conditions. He is really quite cynical about whether human beings can make any meaning out of this endless succession of transitions, all of which have their thresholds.

The second movement in our readings gives us a glimpse of the far side of the threshold, the reality that lies ahead. The text from Revelation says, "See, I am making all things new" (v. 5). Like what? The most central element of all this is that God will dwell with mortals. So it will be a place of no sorrow, no hunger, and no thirst, physically and spiritually (see also Rev 7:16 and Isa 49:10). "To the thirsty I will give water" (21:6b). It's like a fantasy world—too good to be true. Now we are more apprehensive than ever.

The final movement is to take a hard look back. Matthew's Gospel places us at exactly the same location as the Revelation text—the throne of God at the end of this age and the beginning of the next. God asks those who stand at this threshold to take a hard look back at the room from which they have just come. And they find that everything hinges on issues of hunger and thirst! The faithful have seen to the feeding of hungry people and in doing so have demonstrated that the promise of a new world without hunger is no idle fancy but a real possibility. They have provided an assurance that makes it possible to move into the new age with confidence, even in the face of all the apprehension and ambiguity that we feel at the threshold.

The future, after all, is a new heaven and earth, not disconnected from those that God first created with an abundance for all. It also comes as an invitation to all of us to move into the New Year as those who participate in our Lord's life, which he poured out for others, the ones we discover along the margins in our world.

In the mid-1970s, when Bread for the World was still very new, Congress considered the "Right to Food Resolution." Young Congressman Charles Grassley of Iowa was opposed to the resolution. To think that people should have the right to eat if they weren't working for it went against his work ethic and accountability ideals. He graciously accepted the invitation of our fledgling Bread for the World group in the small county-seat town of Waverly to talk about it. That conversation was one of the factors that led Representative Grassley to support the resolution. After all, he also believed Matthew 25; how could it be clearer that everyone, including the least among us, has the right to eat? That resolution has provided the basis for every bit of hunger legislation that has followed. One key element in our ongoing advocacy is to make sure that assistance actually gets to "the least of these," to those most in need.

Children's Time

Think about these quotes from Mother Teresa: "We give our whole-hearted free service to the poorest of the poor. . . . Here in the slums, in the broken body, in the children, we see Christ and we touch him. . . . It is a continual contact with Christ in his work, it is the same contact we have during Mass and in the Blessed Sacrament."[1] How might we explain to children that in the faces of very poor people, in children who lack many of the things we take for granted in our nation, Christ dwells? How can we encourage them in the new year to find fresh ways to embrace their needy neighbors?

Musical Suggestions [LH]

In the Bulb There Is a Flower—NCH 433

Standing at the Future's Threshold—NCH 538

Here Am I—FWS 2178

One Is the Body—GC 846

---

1. Malcolm Muggeridge, *Something Beautiful for God* (New York: Ballantine Books, 1971; San Francisco: Harper & Row, 1973) 97, 114.

Herman Diers

◾

All Saints' Day

◾

RCL: Isaiah 25:6-9; Psalm 24; Revelation 21:1-6a; John 11:32-44
LM: Revelation 7:2-4, 9-14; Psalm 24:1-2, 3-4, 5-6; 1 John 3:1-3;
   Matthew 5:1-12a

Today's readings suggest a series of four topics. The first of these is
visions. The lessons appointed for All Saints' Day point to visions of
life beyond this present existence. The passage from Isaiah invites the
Jews to look beyond their captivity in Babylon to a day of rich feasting
for all peoples, when "the Lord God will wipe away the tears from all
faces" (25:8). Revelation holds up the prospect of a new heaven and a
new earth.

Next, we can look at the effect of visions. One view is that the promise of "pie in the sky by and by" is the perfect escapism because it leaves
hearers feeling that they have no responsibility. God will make everything come out just fine in God's own good time. Without a doubt,
people in power have used this attitude throughout the ages to keep
their subjects in submission, resigned to their fate while they wait for a
deus ex machina deliverance.

This may well have been at the back of the minds of slaveholders
who smiled condescendingly at the singing of Negro spirituals. More
recent study, however, has demonstrated that these spirituals served as
a powerful force for the slaves in maintaining their humanity and carrying on the struggle. Martin Luther King Jr. rallied the energies of
African Americans with his great vision—"I have a dream." He confirmed

the word of the sage, "Where there is no vision, the people perish" (Prov 29:18, KJV).

The third theme is the content of the visions. These include:

- A life of plenty, physically as well as metaphorically. Isaiah envisions "a feast of rich food, a feast of well-aged wines, of rich food filled with marrow, of well-aged wines strained clear" (v. 6). The Revelation vision continues in verse 6b with the promise of water for those who thirst.

- For all people. All of heaven and earth will be made new (Rev 21:1). Isaiah's feast is for all peoples (25:6). Psalm 24 is the great celebration that "the earth is the Lord's and all that is in it, the world and those who live in it" (v. 1).

- New structures—a new heaven and a new earth chief among them.

- At their heart, the notion that death is not the last word. Frederick Buechner affirms that indeed death does not have the last word, because the final word is that we are terribly loved and forgiven.[1] One pregnant thought we have heard more than once is that the true test of a civilization is the quality of life it makes possible for its weakest members. I first heard this from Dr. Richard Foege, formerly a medical missionary and leader of the World Health Organization program to eradicate smallpox and more recently advisor to the Gates Foundation, at a convocation at Wartburg College in September 1987.

The final theme is our response to the vision. In the gospel Jesus responds to this vision at the death of Lazarus. He is so disturbed and moved that for the only recorded time in his life he breaks down in tears. Still, he is not overwhelmed by the powers of death; instead, he defies them by raising Lazarus.

Bread for the World's vision is that world hunger can be cut in half by the year 2015. This, too, calls for acts of defiance in the face of the power of death. It is a vision that embraces all humankind, that satisfies our most elemental human need, and that calls for new structures of justice and generosity. We are invited to join Mother Teresa and St. Francis and the saints of all the ages, past, present, and future, in bringing food and justice to the hungry. Death will not have the last word!

---

1. Frederick Buechner, *The Final Beast* (San Francisco: Harper & Row, 1982).

While on my bicycle pilgrimage to raise awareness for Bread for the World across Washington State and Idaho in 2000, one of the congregations that I visited had suffered immeasurable pain. One high school son of the congregation had been murdered, only to have his brother suffer such grief at this loss that he took his own life. It was devastating. Death seemingly had had the last word not once but twice. And yet the congregation continued to worship—and to feed hungry people in the community. They thoughtfully gave their pastor a brief leave as a time for recovery. I arrived after he had returned, and he enthusiastically welcomed the vision of Bread for the World. Thanks be to God who gives us the victory and the vision.

Children's Time [LH]

This might be a good time to talk about tears. Ask the children if they've ever cried, and why. Say you've cried when something hurt you, and when someone you loved died. Jesus, in today's gospel, cries because a close friend of his, Lazarus, has died. Tears are a way we show we're sad when someone dies. But on days like All Saints' Day, we remember people who have died but not just with sadness. Today we celebrate and are joyful because so many people have walked this earth and really made a difference in our lives—relatives, friends, people in our church, even people we've never met but who followed Jesus and want us to do the same. Thanks be to God for all these people!

Musical Suggestions [LH]

Let Us Be Bread—GC 816

I Want to Be Ready—NCH 616

O Holy City, Seen of John—NCH 613

Time Now to Gather—FWS 2265

Herman Diers

Thanksgiving Day

RCL: Joel 2:21-27; Psalm 126; 1 Timothy 2:1-7; Matthew 6:25-33

LM: Deuteronomy 8:7-18 or 1 Kings 8:55-61 or Sirach 50:22-24 or
  Daniel 6:12-28; Psalm 113:1-8 or Psalm 138:1-5; Colossians 3:12-17
  or 1 Corinthians 1:3-9 or 1 Timothy 6:6-11, 17-19; Mark 5:18-20 or
  Luke 12:15-21 or Luke 17:11-19 or Luke 21:20-28

Thanksgiving is the opposite of arrogance and self-centeredness. It is the recognition that life is a gift. Thanksgiving Day is grounded in this perspective.

Today's passages identify God as the source of this gift. Israel rejoices in the Lord who has restored them, as they remember that God has done great things for them (Ps 126). Even foreign nations recognize this blessing. Now, in hard times, as they sow in tears, that faith provides the basis for their pleas that God will bring them deliverance once more.

New Testament people, looking to Jesus, are caught up in the same song of thanksgiving even when things are difficult. There is plenty of "sowing in tears" (Ps 126:5) for Christians standing with poor people in the struggle for justice, yet always with the hope that they will "reap with shouts of joy" (Ps 126:5) because the Lord continues to do great things.

A second key point in today's passages is that the gift God gives is for all. In the first lesson Joel invites the soil of the earth and the animals of the field to join Zion's children in exalting God. This universality embraces all creation in the thanksgiving of God's people, a reminder that the struggle for justice is never separated from the care of the earth, without which there will be no food or life of any kind.

The theme of universality comes through in the instructions Timothy receives for the life of worship in the congregation. Prayers and thanksgiving are to be offered for everyone. Thanksgiving for everyone? Yes, even for those who are poor—not because they are poor and not because they are the occasions for our "feel-good" generosity, but because they are "Christ in his distressing guise," as Mother Teresa put it.[1]

The text from 1 Timothy specifically encourages prayers for "kings and all who are in high positions" so that we can lead a "quiet and peaceable life in all godliness and dignity" (2:2). This is the basic premise for Christian activism. Those in positions of power have a God-given responsibility to enact policies that will move our nation and the world toward a "quiet and peaceable life" for all. We would be derelict in our discipleship if we did not keep reminding them of this divine responsibility and set before them ways in which they can fulfill it. Bread for the World advocacy campaigns often urge that foreign assistance go to those who are most in need rather than to those who will provide some benefits to us in return. What better investment could there be in a quiet and peaceable life for the world?

In recognizing and enjoying these gifts, we are to avoid stressing out. In the gospel Jesus spells out the transformation of spirit that happens when people realize that life and the things that sustain it (food, drink, and clothing) are gifts from God. Such people are at ease, released from worry and anxiety, because they know that God will provide for them. Jesus puts his finger on a very real temptation of the human spirit—to be greedy and self-centered. Those who seek security in great accumulation and high consumption will never build barns large enough. Any tidbit they may give away would, in their minds, jeopardize their own quality of life.

Elaborate economic theories have been built on the belief that greed and selfishness are the only reliable motivations for prosperity. However, John Nash (from the film "A Beautiful Mind") won the Nobel Prize for demonstrating that even in mathematical terms, those who act out of concern also for the well-being of those around them are most likely to do well themselves.

1. Malcolm Muggeridge, *Something Beautiful for God* (New York: Ballantine Books, 1971; San Francisco: Harper & Row, 1973) 97.

Jesus would free us from anxiety, allowing us to share with others and to advocate on behalf of those who lack food, water, or clothing.

A young, single mother of two from Tacoma's inner-city Hilltop neighborhood returned home with the groceries she had received from a local food bank. It was her allocation for the month. She immediately delivered half of them to her new neighbor, who had not yet established a support system for her family. When asked why she would do such a thing, she could only answer, "They were hungry too." She had the confidence that somehow she could make do. Here is another reason to offer thanksgiving for what we learn about generosity from those who are poor and for the spirit they have to give to us.

Children's Time [LH]

Pick up on Joel's images that the soil and the animals and Zion's people will join forces to praise God. Maybe think about making a holy noise as you ask the children to imagine what it would sound like for dirt and various animals, as well as people, to praise God. Creatively pick some animals that might enjoy the fields and fruit of the trees, and imagine their joyful noise! Then choose one of the many modern praise songs and have the children join in with their "oinks" and "moos" and "baas" (perhaps turkeys can be excused for this particular day).

Musical Suggestions [LH]

Lord of Feasting and of Hunger—BP 141

Great Spirit God—NCH 341

Come and Find the Quiet Center—FWS 2128

We Are Called—GC 718

Contributors

HERMAN DIERS has been a community organizer in the Hilltop, the inner-city community of Tacoma, Washington, for more than a decade, following a career at Wartburg College, first as the chaplain and then as a faculty member. He has been active in Bread for the World since its earliest days. In 2000 he took a four-hundred-mile bicycle tour across Washington State and into Coeur d'Alene, Idaho, stopping at churches along the way to encourage their participation in Bread for the World.

GARNETT E. FOSTER, a pastor of the Presbyterian Church (U.S.A.), is director of field education at Louisville Presbyterian Theological Seminary in Kentucky. She has served multicultural congregations in New Jersey and Maryland. A longtime member of Bread for the World, part of Garnett's heart lies in the Palestinian refugee camps of the West Bank and Gaza.

MARIE HANSELMAN is pastor and choir director of the First Presbyterian Church of Ripley, New York. While Marie was a student at Louisville Presbyterian Theological Seminary in Kentucky, Rev. Garnett Foster invited her to provide musical suggestions for Garnett's contributions to this volume. Marie has a music education degree from the State University of New York at Potsdam and for fifteen years served as music and choir director at the First Presbyterian Church in Victor, New York.

LARRY HOLLAR is senior regional organizer with Bread for the World in its Dayton, Ohio, field office, and formerly served as BFW's issues director. Trained in languages at Williams College, the law at Yale Law School, and biblical interpretation and theology at Wesley

Theological Seminary, he served on the legal staff of a congressional committee and a federal executive department before joining the BFW staff in 1985. He is an ordained elder in the Presbyterian Church (U.S.A.), a professional biblical storyteller and singer, and is editor of this volume.

CURETON L. JOHNSON, D. MIN., is the senior pastor of First (Missionary) Baptist Church in Fayetteville, North Carolina. He was media relations coordinator on the staff of Bread for the World during most of the 1980s. Johnson has served as chairman of CFRBCD, Inc., an HIV/AIDS grassroots outreach project in the Cape Fear region of the state and is currently the executive director of Imani, a mentoring program for African American male youth.

GEORGE S JOHNSON, a Bread for the World activist and member since its early days, was the director of the hunger program for the American Lutheran Church from 1980 to 1987. He is the author of *Beyond Guilt: Christian Response to Suffering,* which is in its third printing. He has served Lutheran parishes in Minnesota and California and taught courses on peace and justice at seminaries in Minnesota, California, and in Africa and India. His degrees are from the School of Theology, Claremont, California, and from Luther Seminary in St. Paul, Minnesota. Johnson now resides in North San Diego County, California, and is director of Third World Opportunities, which coordinates consciousness-raising trips into Mexico.

THE REV. JAMES L. MCDONALD is Bread for the World's vice president for policy and programs, and earlier was a BFW international policy analyst and led its effort to secure debt relief for the world's poorest countries. He has directed the Humphrey Fellowship Program at American University and taught courses in world politics, U.S. foreign policy, and the international relations of Latin America at George Washington University and American University. As a Presbyterian Church (U.S.A.) minister, Jim served congregations in Bloomington, Indiana, Philadelphia, Pennsylvania, and in the Washington, D.C., metropolitan area. He holds degrees from American University, Union Theological Seminary in New York, and Princeton University.

MARC MILLER, a pastor in the Evangelical Lutheran Church in America, received his Master's of Divinity through Christ Seminary-

Seminex in St. Louis and Chicago. He has served parishes in Colorado, Utah, and Ohio, and is currently an Assistant to the Bishop of the Northwest Ohio Synod of the ELCA. In addition to serving as a Bread for the World district coordinator in Utah and Ohio, he also started a Habitat for Humanity chapter in Summit County, Utah.

FATHER MICHAEL SEIFERT is a member of the Atlanta Province of the Marist Fathers. Originally from Alabama, he has worked on the border between Mexico and the U.S. for the past sixteen years. His parish is in Cameron Park, a shantytown just north of Brownsville, Texas, which the 2000 U.S. Census discovered to be the poorest community in the United States. Mike has been involved in Bread for the World activities for many years. His contribution to this volume was nourished by ideas from Father Ruben Becerra, pastor of Nuestro Señor del Rescate parish in Matamoros, Mexico. Father Becerra is active in Proyecto Vida Digna, seeking to provide adequate nutrition to people living on a garbage dump near Matamoros.

MARGUERITE SHUSTER, a Presbyterian Church (U.S.A.) minister, is professor of preaching at Fuller Theological Seminary, where she also teaches systematic theology. Her most recent book is *The Fall and Sin: What We Have Become as Sinners* (Eerdmans, 2004). Previously she served as a pastor for a dozen years in Arcadia and in Pasadena, California. Besides being a longtime member of Bread for the World, she is an avid environmentalist and serves on the board of directors of the Sierra Madre Mountain Conservancy.

GLEN STASSEN is Lewis B. Smedes professor of Christian ethics at Fuller Theological Seminary in Pasadena, California. He has published two books on just peacemaking theory: *Just Peacemaking: Ten Practices for Abolishing War* (Pilgrim Press, 1998 and 2004) and *Just Peacemaking: Transforming Initiatives for Justice and Peace* (Westminster/John Knox Press, 1992). He has also published, with David Gushee, *Kingdom Ethics: Following Jesus in Contemporary Context* (InterVarsity Press, 2003). Stassen invites students in his classes to join Bread for the World after reading Ron Sider's book *Rich Christians in an Age of Hunger* and learning about the excellent work of Bread for the World and of his students who have gone to work for Bread for the World.

DR. MICHELLE TOOLEY is Eli Lilly professor of religious ethics at Berea College in Berea, Kentucky. Previously she taught women's studies in religion and Christian social ethics at Belmont University in Nashville, Tennessee. Her book *Voices of the Voiceless* describes the struggle for justice of women in human rights groups in Guatemala. She has been a local group leader and campus activist as well as board member for Bread for the World, and is vice chair of the board of directors of Witness for Peace.

REV. ELIZABETH VANDER HAAGEN is a pastoral resident at Church of the Servant Christian Reformed Church in Grand Rapids, Michigan. She attended Calvin College, Princeton Theological Seminary, and Calvin Theological Seminary. As a Bread for the World activist, she helped organize letter-writing activities at Calvin Seminary.

SISTER CHRISTINE VLADIMIROFF, O.S.B., is a professed member of the Benedictine Sisters of Erie. She was elected prioress of the monastic community in 1998 and currently serves in that position. More recently she was elected to serve the Leadership Conference of Women Religious as vice-president, president, and past president sequentially during the years 2003–2006. She was president and CEO of America's Second Harvest National Network of Food Banks from 1991 to 1998. Sister Christine has served on the Bread for the World board of directors, chairing the board from 2000 to 2002. She has a doctorate in Latin American Studies and has done graduate work in Scripture and theology.

FATHER CLARENCE WILLIAMS, C.PP.S., PH.D., is a member of the Missionaries of the Precious Blood and director of the Office for Black Catholic Ministries for the Archdiocese of Detroit. He directs the Institute for Recovery from Racisms and is co-convener of Building Bridges in Black and Brown, a national dialogue between the African American and Hispano/Latino communities. Father Clarence also is president of the Catholic African World Network communications ministry. He has pastored a local parish in Detroit, served as vice chairperson of Bread for the World's board of directors, and offered training in the area of communications and racial sobriety with Bread for the World's staff.

Bread for the World

BREAD FOR THE WORLD is a 55,000-member Christian citizens' movement against hunger. Founded in 1974, Bread for the World's members lobby Congress and the Administration to bring about public policy
changes that address the root causes of hunger and poverty in the United
States and overseas. BREAD FOR THE WORLD is a nonpartisan organization supported by 45 denominations and many theological perspectives. For more information, call 1-800-82-BREAD or see the
movement's website, www.bread.org.

Scripture Index

The following index includes references to the readings of both the Revised Common Lectionary and the Lectionary for Mass, listing the more inclusive passage where readings differ. Page citations, given after the slash (/) mark, refer to the first page of the reflection for the day the passage appears. Writers sometimes do not address each passage assigned for that day, so the reader may not find a comment on that passage in the day's reflection.